Ethics for Disaster

Studies in Social, Political, and Legal Philosophy

Series Editor: James P. Sterba, University of Notre Dame

This long-standing Rowman & Littlefield philosophy series critically analyzes and evaluates the major social, political, and legal ideals, institutions, and practices of our time. **James P. Sterba**, past president of the American Philosophical Association's Central Division, and widely known and respected public philosopher throughout the world, brings dynamic, leading voices to bear on important and provocative topics, demonstrating the value of philosophical thinking in responding to contemporary issues.

Titles

Necessary Goods: Our Responsibilities to Meet Others Needs (1998),
    edited by Gillian Brock
Living in Integrity: A Global Ethic to Restore a Fragmented Earth (1998)
    by Laura Westra
Approximate Justice: Studies in Social, Political, and Legal Philosophy (1998)
    by George Sher
Character and Culture (1997)
    by Lester H. Hunt
Cowboy Metaphysics: Ethics and Death in Westerns (1997)
    by Peter A. French
Partisan or Neutral? The Futility of Public Political Theory (1997)
    by Michael White
Nature as Subject: Human Obligation and Natural Community (1996)
    by Eric Katz
Can Ethics Provide Answers? And Other Essays in Moral Philosophy (1996)
    by James Rachels
Perfect Equality: John Stuart Mill on Well-Constituted Communities (1996)
    by Maria H. Morales
Citizenship in a Fragile World (1996)
    by Bernard P. Dauenhauer
Plato Rediscovered: Human Value and Social Order (1996)
    by T. K. Seung
In the Company of Others: Perspectives on Community, Family, and Culture (1996),
    edited by Nancy E. Snow
Critical Moral Liberalism: Theory and Practice (1996)
    by Jeffrey Reiman
For and Against the State: New Philosophical Readings (1996),
    edited by John T. Sanders and Jan Narveson
Moral Rights and Political Freedom (1995)
    by Tara Smith
The Individual and the Value of Human Life (1995)
    by Joseph Popper-Lynkeus
Contract Ethics: Evolutionary Biology and the Moral Sentiments (1995)
    by Howard Kahane
Capitalism with a Human Face: The Quest for a Middle Road in Russian Politics (1995)
    by William Gay and T. A. Alekseeva
Punishment as Societal-Defense (1995)
    by Phillip Montague
Faces of Environmental Racism: Confronting Issues of Global Justice (1995),
    edited by Laura Westra and Peter S. Wenz
Critical Legal Theory and the Challenge of Feminism:
  A Philosophical Reconception (1994)
    by Matthew H. Kramer
Morality and Social Justice: Point/Counterpoint (1994)
    by James P. Sterba, Alison M. Jaggar, Carol C. Gould, Robert C. Solomon,
    Tibor R. Machan, William A. Galston, and Milton Fisk
An Environmental Proposal for Ethics: The Principle of Integrity (1994)
    by Laura Westra
On the Eve of the 21st Century: Perspectives of Russian and
  American Philosophers (1994),
    edited by William C. Gay and T. A. Alekseeva

The Liberalism-Communitarianism Debate (1994),
    edited by C. F. Delaney
Marx and Modern Political Theory: From Hobbes to Contemporary Feminism (1993)
    by Philip J. Kain
Patriotism, Morality, and Peace (1993)
    by Stephen Nathanson
*Collective Responsibility: Five Decades of Debate in Theoretical and
    Applied Ethics* (1991),
        edited by Larry May and Stacey Hoffman
Social Contract Theories: Political Obligation or Anarchy (1990)
    by Vicente Medina

Ethics for Disaster

Naomi Zack

ROWMAN & LITTLEFIELD PUBLISHERS, INC.
Lanham • Boulder • New York • Toronto • Plymouth, UK

ROWMAN & LITTLEFIELD PUBLISHERS, INC.

Published in the United States of America
by Rowman & Littlefield Publishers, Inc.
A wholly owned subsidary of The Rowman & Littlefield Publishing Group, Inc.
4501 Forbes Boulevard, Suite 200, Lanham, Maryland 20706
www.rowmanlittlefield.com

Estover Road
Plymouth PL6 7PY
United Kingdom

British Library Cataloguing in Publication Information Available

Library of Congress Cataloging-in-Publication Data:

Zack, Naomi, 1944–
   Ethics for disaster / Naomi Zack.
      p. cm. — (Studies in social, political, and legal philosophy)
   Includes bibliographical references (p.   ) and index.
   ISBN 978-0-7425-6494-7 (cloth : alk. paper) — ISBN 978-0-7425-6496-1
(electronic)
   1. Emergency management—Moral and ethical aspects. 2. Disasters. 3. Risk
assessment. I. Title.
   HV551.2.Z33 2009
   172'.2—dc22   2008052261

Printed in the United States of America

♾™ The paper used in this publication meets the minimum requirements of
American National Standard for Information Sciences—Permanence of Paper for
Printed Library Materials, ANSI/NISO Z39.48-1992.

To my sons, Alexander Linden Erdmann
and
Bradford Zack Mahon

Because something is happening here
And you don't know what it is,
Do you, Mr. Jones?

—Bob Dylan, "Ballad of a Thin Man," 1965

Never let the future disturb you. You will meet it, if you have to, with the same weapons of reason which today arm you against the present.

—Marcus Aurelius, *Meditations*, AD 200

Contents

Preface

BACKGROUND TO THE BOOK

Twelve times in the past sixteen years, I have taught a large introduction-to-ethics course (at the University at Albany, State University of New York, from 1991 to 2001 and at the University of Oregon from 2002 to the present). These classes typically contain over two hundred students. My teaching assistants grade the required short essays and conduct weekly discussion groups of twenty to thirty students. The course first introduces students to moral arguments and then presents the classic moral systems of *Consequentialism*, *Deontology*, and *Virtue Ethics*. I often use examples from literature and film. I always maintain an interactive classroom, encouraging student discussion.

Intellectually, the lecture material for the large class is not difficult to prepare, but delivering it requires a willingness to learn. Many students in these introductory classes are surprised by the degree and intensity of disagreement among philosophers concerning basic moral values and principles. At first, many find it challenging to come up with reasons and arguments for their own opinions. Their perplexity has motivated me to articulate my own perplexity, and their understandable confusions have set a high standard of clarity for my own speech and writing. Figuring out how to teach ethics in a way that encourages students to develop their own principled perspectives has been my best preparation for writing this book.

However, I did not recognize the moral aspects of disaster immediately. I first became interested in the subject through media reports following Hurricane Katrina. What I saw then resulted in a new kind of fear for me and a new anxious prudence. After Katrina, government officials all over the

United States were repeatedly interviewed on television regarding disasters specific to their regions. When public health personnel in New York City spoke about what to do in the event of a nuclear attack, they instructed the lay public on how to decontaminate themselves and stay upwind of radioactive "plumes." The mayor of San Francisco advised his audience that the city had not been adequately retrofitted for the next major earthquake, which was surely coming. There were new documentaries on the probability of a major earthquake in the Pacific Northwest, due anytime within the next fifty years. Informational films were also shown in local venues throughout the United States. All of the interviews, predictions, depictions of disasters, and warnings, as well as the ongoing story of Hurricane Katrina, were accompanied by official messages to the public, which amounted to this:

> *Professional emergency personnel cannot respond immediately. In the event of disaster, you will be on your own for anytime between three days and two weeks. You need to prepare.*

My understanding and processing of this message, as a private member of the public, constituted my initial approach to the subject of disaster. I assembled disaster kits and, since I live in Oregon, bought earthquake insurance. In the fall of 2005, I attended a Eugene city club meeting about local disaster preparation. At that meeting, I met Dr. Christopher Bellavita, senior editor of the online journal *Homeland Security Affairs*. He asked me what the philosophical approach to contemporary disasters was. I did not have an answer, but I began to think about it. What, if anything, can a philosopher contribute to the subject of disaster?

Combining what I considered philosophically relevant with my underlying amateur practical perspective, I wrote an article, "Philosophy and Disaster," published in the April 2006 issue of *Homeland Security Affairs*.[1] This gave me ideas for a new course, "The Philosophy of Disaster and Emergency Response." During the spring of 2006, I took a twenty-five-hour Citizens Emergency Response Team (CERT) course, which provided training in light search and rescue, basic first aid, and the use of small fire extinguishers; I followed this with enrollment in a "Train the Trainer" course at a national CERT conference in Los Angeles.[2] I thought that this practical training would help anchor new theoretical work, in addition to having personal (amateur) usefulness.

Also in the spring of 2006, I was a guest at a meeting about pandemics convened by an emergency task force representing medical professionals in Lane County. Two current articles served to focus the subject of the meeting. The first, "Concept of Operations for Triage of Mechanical Ventilation in an Epidemic," was published by the Society for Academic Emergency

Medicine. The second, "Medical Countermeasures for Pandemic Influenza: Ethics and the Law," was published by the *Journal of the American Medical Association*.[3] Both articles discussed the likely shortage of ventilators for acute respiratory distress in a flu pandemic and proposed triage models. The models consisted of treatment criteria levels based on patients' future life-year prognoses and likelihood of recovery. Their maxim was, *Treat those who will benefit most from treatment and live longest as a result.* However, public officials and personnel employed in vital services would also get priority. Although defining cut-off ages was admitted to be difficult, the ill and elderly were characterized as less eligible to receive treatment than those who were healthy and young. (At the first medical task force meeting I attended it was also noted in discussion that infants would not be transported for treatment.)

The first article proposed that in some instances, it would be permissible to withdraw mechanical ventilation from patients who were expected to survive with treatment for reallocation to those higher up on the triage list. The article with the ethics subtitle took it as a foregone conclusion that extreme emergency conditions require something more than the random allocation of treatment called for by "blind fairness." The overarching ethical principle invoked was "Save the Greatest Number," but even that principle was presented as dispensable given the urgency of saving the socially useful and the young. Both models contained provisions for the legal indemnification of officials who instituted the triage and the medical personnel who carried it out. I thought that there was something deeply wrong morally with this entire picture, but I still did not see the entire subject of disaster preparation and response in moral terms.

A year later, I taught "The Philosophy of Disaster and Emergency Response" for the first time. The course focused on the practical issues of preparation, response, and mitigation, supplemented by philosophical readings. However, as the term went on, moral questions became increasingly prominent in lectures and discussions. I realized that I had strong intuitions about what should and should not be done in planning and responding to disaster and that many of the students shared them. Furthermore, it became plain that the only proof we could offer for the validity of our intuitions was that others shared them. There is no way to "prove" the value of human life or the principles that we ought to treat each other fairly and not harm one another. We accept such principles, and the value of human life that they presuppose, as basic requirements for enjoying our own lives and living in society.

Philosophically, I came to the conclusion that if we have to live through disasters, we should not too easily give up our ordinary moral intuitions, before the fact, while there is still time to plan. And that's the main thesis of this book.

This book aims to bring moral reflection to bear on the broad multidisciplinary and multipractice field of disaster. I use the word "moral" to make a contrast against the tendency to attach the term "ethics" to new sets of emergency rules and protocols, without discussion or reflection on whether they are right or just. But philosophers and others use "morality" and "ethics" interchangeably, and that will be my practice here.

In planning for disaster, or deciding that such planning can be deferred, there can be open discussions or closed ones. Open discussions would involve the public and professional ethicists, who are not practitioners in the field in which ethics are at stake. Closed discussions can involve anyone with sufficient power and authority and could lead to any decision at all, without full examination of relevant moral presuppositions or even of the consequences of what is concluded. Closed discussion is the default option at present and is likely to result in investigation and punishment, after the fact, when it is too late for those whose survival was not made a priority.

Philosophy has no established role in an ethics for disaster. Disinterested ethical discussion about disaster preparation and response is just as new to philosophy as it apparently is in current public policy contexts. For a long time, academic philosophers have used examples from so-called *lifeboat ethics* in the same way they've used science fiction. Extreme scenarios are posited to show the undesirable implications of opponents' moral systems. This throw-away quality of lifeboat ethics is based on a long-standing premise in Western political philosophy that morality and justice only begin when there is government to regulate and organize society. The premise was Plato's starting point in *The Republic*, when Socrates suggested that the difficulties of defining justice as a virtue stemmed from the smallness of individuals. Socrates's solution was to examine the individual "writ large" in the form of the state. In the seventeenth century, Thomas Hobbes stipulated that there could be no justice without government (which he also conceived as a huge individual in *Leviathan*). And in the eighteenth century, David Hume assumed that orderly society was a precondition for justice. His words could have been written for a type of early-twenty-first-century crisis thinking, which assumes that when ordinary life is suspended, ordinary morals are also suspended:

> Suppose a society to fall into such want of all common necessities, that the utmost frugality and industry cannot preserve the greater number from perishing, and the whole from extreme misery: It will readily, I believe, be admitted that the strict laws of justice are suspended in such a pressing emergence, and give place to the stronger motives of necessity and self-preservation. Is it any crime, after a shipwreck, to seize whatever means or instrument of safety one can lay hold of, without regard to former limitations of property? Or if a city besieged were perishing with hunger; can we imagine, that men will see any

means of preservation, before them, and lose their lives, from a scrupulous re-gard to what, in other situations, would be the rules of equity and justice?[4]

Many of us who live in the rich parts of the world enjoy relatively secure, normal everyday lives. This is both a primary value in itself and a source of values. When we think about disaster, as a disruption of such normality, we owe it to ourselves and others not to lose sight of the fact that our ordinary, safe life is an attained human ideal. This attained ideal is a value we are ob-ligated to preserve as intellectuals as well as human beings.

NOTES

1. Naomi Zack, "Philosophy and Disaster," *Homeland Security Affairs* 2, no. 1, art. 5 (2006): 1–2 (www.hsaj.org/?article=2.1.5).
2. CERT is funded by the Federal Emergency Management Agency (FEMA), which is now part of the Department of Homeland Security.
3. J. Hick and D. O'Laughlin, "Concept of Operations for Triage of Mechanical Ventilation in an Epidemic," *Academic Emergency Medicine* 13 (2006): 223–29; L. Gostin, "Medical Countermeasures for Pandemic Influenza: Ethics and the Law," *JAMA* 295 (2006): 554–56. (I discuss these articles more systematically in chapter 4.)
4. David Hume, "Of Justice," in *An Inquiry Concerning the Principles of Morals* (In-dianapolis, IN: Hackett, 1983), 22–23.

Acknowledgments

I am grateful to Dr. Christopher Bellavita for asking the question that started me thinking about disaster in philosophical terms. That question led to the article that became the starting point for my academic project: "Philosophy and Disaster" (*Homeland Security* Affairs 2, no. 1, art. 5, April 2006, www.hsaj.org/?article=2.1.5). I am also grateful to Geoff Simmons MD, program manager for the Citizens Emergency Response Team (CERT) in Eugene, Oregon. The practical, hands-on aspects of disaster preparation and response, which he teaches, have grounded my theoretical work. I thank Jenny Soyke, MD, for including me in Lane County medical personnel discussions on pandemic preparations in 2006 and 2007, as well as for both her open-mindedness and that of the audience.

Because a philosophical contribution is necessarily less practical and less specialized than that of those who directly work with or think about the physical reality of disaster, contact with the activities and discourse of those practitioners helps keep the philosophical contribution relevant. When I taught the new course, Philosophy of Disaster and Emergency Response, at the University of Oregon in the spring of 2007 and 2008, I based part of the final grade on student commitment to learning a new emergency skill, such as CPR or CERT training. Overall, I learned from my students about how to present and develop this subject, not just philosophically but from a humanities perspective more generally. And hearing about the specific skills they acquired expanded my own knowledge. My graduate student teaching assistants, John Kaag (2007) and Jason Jordan (2008), did much to stimulate discussion and help explain philosophical ideas and methods to students from a wide range of academic majors. John and Jason also encouraged me in the development of this book. My research for the course development itself, including CERT training, conference travel, and hosting outside classroom speakers, was supported by a generous award from the University of Oregon Tom and Carol Williams Fund for Undergraduate Education. I am also grateful to the University of Oregon and the Philosophy Department for sabbatical leave during the fall of 2007 and winter of 2008, which allowed me to concentrate on earlier drafts and revisions of the manuscript for this book.

Audience and commentator response to papers representing earlier versions of the ideas developed here were invaluable at the following times and places. I presented "Race, Class, and Money in Disaster," which is chapter 6 herein, at the Spindel Conference, "Race, Racism, and Liberalism in the 21st Century," at the University of Memphis in September 2008 (scheduled for publication in a forthcoming special supplement to the *Southern Journal of Philosophy*). At the Eastern Division meeting of the American Philosophical Association (APA) in December 2007, I presented papers on disaster documentaries and teaching my disaster course, which both became part of the introduction to this book. In September 2007, I gave a version of the first parts of chapter 4, "Social Contract Theory and Disaster Preparation," at the Conference on Democracy, Liberalism, and Pragmatism at Constantin Brancusi University, Targu-Jiu, Romania (scheduled for publication in *International Perspectives on Pragmatism*, ed. Cerasel Cuteanu, Cambridge, UK, Cambridge Scholars, 2009, 33–46). In July 2007, I gave at talk titled "The Ethics of Disaster Preparation" at a Philosophy of Management conference at St. Anne's College, Oxford, UK. That talk contained the main parts of what is now chapter 1 and is scheduled for publication in *Philosophy of Management* (Special Issue, *Ethics of Crisis*, ed. Per Sandin, autumn/winter, 2008–2009, 7.3). In the spring of 2007, I presented an early draft of chapter 6, called "Identities, Historical Explanation and Disaster," at a memorial session for Iris Young at the APA Pacific meeting in San Francisco and at the University of Oregon in a Center for Race, Ethnicity and Sexuality Studies seminar organized by its director, Michael Hames-García.

I talked about the main ideas concerning John Locke and social contract theory to a group of highly motivated students at Washington and Lee University, Lexington, Virginia, in the spring of 2007. In winter 2007, I benefited from comments by my Philosophy Department colleagues on my *Homeland Security Affairs* article during a faculty workshop. Special thanks to Scott Pratt, John Lysaker, Mark Johnson, and Cheyney Ryan. I also talked about social contract theory and the role of government in civilian emergency response in several contexts in 2006, including at the APA Pacific meeting in San Francisco and at "Spelling Disaster," a conference at Portland State University.

Thanks to numerous graduate students in the University of Oregon Philosophy Department for ongoing discussion about this subject, especially

Jazmine Gabriel, who proofread an earlier version of the manuscript and prepared the bibliography in December 2007, and Jason Jordan for also reading that earlier version and later reminding me of the Lisbon earthquake of 1755. Thanks also to Tomas Hulick Baiza, on whose doctoral dissertation committee in the School of Education I served, for suggesting I read Cormac McCarthy's *The Road*, which became a substantial resource for chapter 3.

I am grateful to James Sterba for including this book in his Rowman & Littlefield series, Studies in Social, Political, and Legal Philosophy; I thank Ross Miller for expert editorial advice (and consent), while he was its editor; thanks also to Evan Wiig for his editorial and production assistance, to Elaine McGarraugh for production management, and to Jennifer Kelland Fagan for copyediting. Without their suggestions and assistance, the book would lack its present coherence and clarity. I am indebted to Rowman & Littlefield's external reviewers for stalwart encouragement, as well as many detailed suggestions that have contributed to the strengths of this book, and of course, to Jonathan Sisk for his steady hand at the helm of R&L ever since I first published with the press in 1995. The failings and errors that remain are wholly my own.

Naomi Zack
Eugene, Oregon
December 21, 2008

Introduction and Overview
of the Chapters

WHAT ARE DISASTERS?

In answering this question, it is useful to start by simply pointing to some recent disasters as the term is intelligible to a broad contemporary, and perhaps primarily American, audience. In June 2008, Infoplease, a commercial source of factual information, listed the following events on its website for world disasters during the first half of the year.[1] In January, riots between the Luo and Kikuyu tribes in Kenya resulted in the deaths of over 300 people and extensive property damage; tornados killed 4 people and destroyed property in the Midwestern United States; snowstorms affected 78 million, resulting in 24 deaths in eastern and southern China. In February, two earthquakes in the Democratic Republic of the Congo killed more than 45 people and injured 450; tornados in Tennessee, Arkansas, Alabama, Kentucky, and Missouri resulted in 55 deaths; a passenger-plane crash in Venezuela killed all 46 aboard. In March, tornados in Georgia killed 2 and injured 30; 13 died and hundreds were evacuated due to floods extending from Texas to Pennsylvania. In April, a dengue fever outbreak in Brazil that had begun in January infected over 75,000, with 90 deaths; in Virginia, 3 tornados injured over 200 people and destroyed 140 homes. In May, 7 died and 13 were injured by storms in Arkansas; Cyclone Nargis struck the Irrawaddy Delta and Yangon in Myanmar, killing 78,000, mostly due to a 12-foot-high tidal wave; tornados in Oklahoma and Georgia killed 20 and injured hundreds; 67,000 died and hundreds of thousands were injured during a 7.9 magnitude earthquake in western China, and 150,000 people were evacuated from the Sichus Province to escape floods. In June, flooding in Indiana, Iowa, Illinois, and other Midwestern states killed 10; a tornado

1

killed 4 Boy Scouts in Iowa and two people in Kansas; 60 people in south-ern China died from floods that destroyed 5.4 million acres of crops; in the Philippines, Typhoon Fenshen struck a ferry, killing over 500 people.

Many definitions of disaster abound, but a core consensus holds that a disaster involves great harm to a large number of people. Still, the term also legitimately applies to sudden harm, death, or property destruction where fewer lives are lost. In the above listing of world disasters, it is striking that single-digit deaths in the United States are listed alongside events resulting in tens of thousands of deaths in Asia. Aside from the way in which such a catalog of recent world disasters seems to privilege the United States, it highlights the disruptive and unexpected nature of events meriting the term *disaster*.

Cyclone Nargis and the earthquake that struck western China stand out as severe natural disasters on a scale comparable to the 2004 Pacific Rim tsunami that killed over 260,000.[2] But from an American perspective, these events unfortunately evoke a sense that disasters happen in far-away na-tions, typically outside of Europe as well as North America. This distance is more than geographical in a global age of instant communication and very fast travel. Even though recent disasters in Asia have evoked compassion and humanitarian aid from the more affluent or technologically nimble North and West, they retain a moral distance in failing to impose a sense of urgent obligation on those who remain relatively safe. The Asian disasters in May 2008 did not receive ongoing, "front-page" media attention in the United States, and many educated Americans were simply unaware of them.

Moral or ethical issues pertain to human well-being. We have a general moral obligation not to harm others and to help those in distress. The ob-ligation becomes more specific when those who require our assistance are already in our care, for example, family members, and that specificity of ob-ligation extends to neighbors, coworkers, and members of the same (geo-graphical, religious, or ethnic) community, state, nation, allied nation, and so forth.

Despite our somewhat self-centered general response to the misfortunes of others, our distress at harm to others and felt obligation to assist them seems to increase in intensity and urgency when misfortunes are unexpected and victims are clearly innocent. There have always been disasters in human history, but the morally compelling apprehension of the innocence of disas-ter victims is relatively new, forcefully emerging during the eighteenth-century European Enlightenment. The Enlightenment enshrined the powers of human reason not merely for scientific and technological exploration, dis-covery, and invention but also as a moral tool. There was growing confidence that human, as well as natural, events were in principle comprehensible. Thus, it was assumed that if an omnipotent, benevolent, and just God existed, the moral reasons for undeserved catastrophe ought to be evident to observers.

On November 1, 1755, an earthquake that experts now believe must have measured 9 on the Richter scale, demolished the city of Lisbon, killing over ninety thousand. The Lisbon earthquake of 1755 became a focal point for the disturbing question of how a good God could allow the innocent to suffer; moreover, it began to corrode an optimistic perspective that this was the best of all possible worlds and that the history of human life was a never-ending story of progress.

In his "Poem on the Lisbon Disaster; Or an Examination of the Axiom 'All Is Well,'" Voltaire first protested the optimistic legacies of Gottfried Leibniz and Alexander Pope:

> Deluded philosophers who cry, "All is well,"
> Hasten, contemplate these frightful ruins,
> This wreck, these shreds, these wretched ashes of the dead

Voltaire then raised the question of the good and powerful deity permitting undeserved harm, also known as "the problem of evil":

> Will you say: "This is result of eternal laws
> Directing the acts of a free and good God!"
> . . .
> What crime, what error did these children,
> Crushed and bloody on their mothers' breasts commit?
> Did Lisbon, which is no more, have more vices
> Than London and Paris immersed in their pleasures?
> Lisbon is destroyed, and they dance in Paris![3]

Jean-Jacques Rousseau soon responded to Voltaire on a number of points. First and foremost, he insisted, "God has done no better for mankind because He can do no better." Rousseau then claimed that human beings are the source of their own moral evils and that the citizens of Lisbon had built seven-story houses in densely populated areas, so many could not flee. Rousseau also conjectured that some had not fled at the first tremors because they were trying to save their possessions. Moreover, he found further reassurance in the thought that many of those who died may have escaped ongoing lives of great misery.[4]

Sebastiao de Melo, the Marquis de Pombal, was prime minister of Portugal at the time of the Lisbon earthquake. He took immediate action to bury the dead, thereby preventing an epidemic, and oversaw reconstruction, including the erection of perhaps the first earthquake-resistant buildings in Europe. Overall, the Lisbon earthquake had major significance for the modern conception of disaster. The themes it evoked—of innocent suffering, pessimism about world events, insecurity, inequality, responsibility, and the need to prepare for and adequately respond to disaster—remain vital today.[5]

Before explaining how these themes are developed in the following chapters, it might be helpful to refer to "term of art" verbal definitions of disasters. We should also be able to distinguish disasters from other mass misfortunes that fall under the category of *risk*, thereby perhaps arriving at a conceptually robust definition of disaster.

According to Red Cross/Red Crescent, "disasters are exceptional events which suddenly kill or injure large numbers of people." The Center for Research on the Epidemiology of Disasters (CRED) in Brussels, Belgium, uses this definition: "A disaster is a situation or event which overwhelms local capacity, necessitating a request to a national or international level for external assistance."[6] CRED's stipulation that disasters require external assistance expresses the perspective of policy makers, emergency practitioners, and others who design and implement disaster assistance. The cost to affected individuals and the disruptions to their normal lives, as well as their responsibility before and after being affected by disaster, provide different perspectives. Indeed, once the psychic dimensions of disasters are considered, it becomes evident that the official definitions of disaster are somewhat superficial.

The distinction between disasters and other large-scale calamities with dire consequences for small or large numbers rests on the degree of danger that is acceptable in normal, nondisastrous life. Such built-in normal danger is now understood to be a matter of *risk* rather than disaster. For example, the worldwide AIDS epidemic, projected to result in eighteen million orphans in Africa by 2010, is not officially considered a disaster, whereas an Avian Flu pandemic is, or would be.[7] Building on Ulrich Brick's 1992 *Risk Society*, some social critics now distinguish between earlier modern ideas that everything is in principle predictable and current everyday circumstances in which many technological advances have new, undeterminable potential for danger.[8] Such insight recognizes a pervasiveness of risk, although risk is not generally considered to be the same thing as disaster.

A very strong and clear example of the difference between risk and disaster is evident in comparisons between contemporary disasters and vehicular accidents. In "Road Kill," an *LA Times* op-ed piece that appeared on August 5, 2007, Greg Easterbrook, a fellow of the Brookings Institution, pointed out that since 9/11, 245,000 Americans had died in road accidents. Worldwide, the figure was six million.[9] By 2012, another six million worldwide and another quarter million in the United States will have died on the road. The combination of a Hurricane Katrina and a mass terrorist attack every year, along with an ongoing Iraq-type war, would not result in as many untimely deaths. Easterbrook suggests plausible reasons for our indifference to traffic fatalities compared to terrorism: the automobile industry thrives on competition for greater horsepower every year; fatal car accidents, although preventable, are not criminal offenses "against morality or human dignity." Moreover, more people than ever now have cars, population grows denser, and laws against cell phone use by drivers are not enforced.[10]

Extending Easterbrook's analysis, there are several additional differences between terrorism and automobile fatalities. First, terrorist events and other disasters are much harder to predict than the frequencies of vehicular accidents. Second, terrorism and other disasters evoke a degree of fear in those who can be affected, which does not accompany automobile use. Third, and most importantly, automobile accidents are part of ordinary, normal life, while in the United States, terrorist events are not.

From 2002 to 2007, there were 192 H5N1 avian influenza deaths, compared to six million global traffic deaths. Death by avian influenza is no less "accidental," or more demeaning, than death on the highway. Neither can it be argued that fear of Avian Flu enriches drug companies in a way that lack of fear of automobiles enriches car makers, because the biggest problem in Avian Flu preparation is insufficient vaccine and treatment medication; that is, the drug companies are unable to make enough money from it.[11] While public fears of Avian Flu have not intensified to the extent that fears of terrorism have, Avian Flu nonetheless became part of the post-9/11 landscape of contemporary disasters in a way that traffic death never has.

Why is there such a difference in fear? One reason is that Avian Flu and Terrorism are already fully loaded in representational ways that traffic death is not. Both Avian Flu viruses and terrorists already represent objects to be feared—exotic disease and demonic foreigners—whereas automobiles, although statistically far more dangerous, are useful, beautiful, and pleasant to own and operate. The distance to death from the existence of terrorists and the H5N1 virus is presumed to be shorter than that from owning, driving, and riding in a Prius, Hummer, or SUV. There is also the near-simultaneity of mass deaths from the same cause in any one Avian Flu pandemic or any one successful terrorist action, whereas road deaths occur singly, or in small numbers, in isolated, uniquely contextualized cases.

Another striking aspect of the difference in fear centers on the *cathectic* nature of Terrorism and Avian Flu. Both can quickly ignite mass fears. The same was true about the anthrax outbreaks after 9/11. These are all *hot fears*. Hot fears are popular—attractive and common. They spread rapidly by contagion, when the mere presence of fear in others is a reason to be afraid oneself. Hot fears may represent deeper or earlier psychic fears, otherwise unexpressed. Their objects may also represent things for which it is normally inappropriate to express fear. A classic example in American life is an ethic or racial group that is privately demonized by a majority otherwise publicly committed to social equality; on the other side, fear of the majority by the devalued groups may rise to paranoia.

The difference in fear between traffic deaths and post-9/11 disasters may be the precise distinction between the kind of risk that the public is able to incorporate into normal life and the nature of contemporary disaster. While not as totally destructive of ordinary life as ongoing war, disaster has a capacity to disrupt normality that goes beyond factual loss of life and destruction of property and physical environments. Ordinary life has become replete with previously unimagined risks (an "obesity epidemic," for example), but disaster has a dramatic dimension that is immediately moral in distinct ways. In between risk-laden ordinary life and disasters that evoke hot fears are natural catastrophes, such as fires, floods, storms, earthquakes, the ominously changing conditions associated with global warming, and impending shortages of vital resources, such as water. While these events do not evoke the same panic as terrorism or avian-influenza–type pandemics and are not as unpredictable, in their actual and imagined destruction, as well as the historical record, they unquestionably qualify as disasters.

WHAT IS A *DISASTER?*

We have so far directly considered several disasters, entertained cursory official definitions of disaster, and reflected on a fear-based psychic distinction between actuarially predictable risk in normal life and contemporary disasters. Historically known and foreseeable disasters also include natural catastrophes and their aftermath. Is it possible on this basis to construct a conceptually comprehensive definition of disaster? A philosopher might (and will soon here) venture to do so, but it should first be noted that there is disagreement concerning methodology and the standpoint of inquiry among social science experts in contemporary disaster research. E. L. Quarantelli, who founded the Disaster Research Center at the University of Delaware in 1963, recognizes three different core concepts of disaster that emerged from the articles in his 1998 anthology *What Is a Disaster?* The first conception is that a disaster is an objectively real event that is known by "piecing together" different perspectives and observations, on the model of blind men touching an elephant. Second, a disaster is a contested social construction that researchers compete to define via different theories of disaster as a social construction. And third, a disaster is of necessity subjectively defined in varied ways, based as much on victims' views as on the views of researchers.[12]

The tension between the ideas that events exist that objectively and universally count as disasters and that what counts as a disaster is relative to other cultural factors suggests that the term *disaster* is value laden as well as political.

To call an event a "disaster" is to signal that it is worthy of immediate, serious human attention and purposive corrective activity; to view an event or condition as problematic in ways other than disastrous is to relegate it to less immediate attention—or neglect. It is evident from these considerations that when disaster-research specialists engage in definitions of disaster, they are embarked on projects of determining what ought to count as disasters and who ought to make such determinations. The resolution of those questions will determine not only what the specialists want to study but what they will be funded and employed to study.

As an amateur observer and possible disaster victim, as well as an ethicist, my job, in comparison with that of the disaster-research specialists, is much more "after the fact." The observer/possible victim indirectly or directly experiences those disruptive events that will have already been designated "disasters." As Quarantelli describes this view, "I cannot define disaster, but I know it when I see it."[13] The ethicist comments on the moral issues attending those predesignated "disasters." And so, for the purposes of this book, a disaster can be defined as follows:

> A *disaster* is an event (or series of events) that harms or kills a significant number of people or otherwise severely impairs or interrupts their daily lives in civil society. Disasters may be natural or the result of accidental or deliberate human action. Disasters include, but are not limited to, fires; floods; storms; earthquakes; chemical spills; leaks of, or infiltration by, toxic substances; terrorist attacks by conventional, nuclear, or biological weapons; epidemics; pandemics; mass failures in electronic communications; and other events that officials and experts designate "disasters." Disasters always occasion surprise and shock; they are unwanted by those affected by them, although not always unpredictable. Disasters also generate narratives and media representations of the heroism, failures, and losses of those who are affected and respond.

This definition leaves room to argue critically for inclusion in the "disaster" category of ongoing disruptive events that have not yet been designated "disasters." The definition leaves out what is known in the disaster literature as events and situations of "conflict." The effects of war on civilian populations may constitute disasters, although from the standpoint of members of the military, wars have deliberate agency, systematic planning, and the active involvement of legitimate government, all of which distinguish them from disasters. Because they are structured, wars more closely resemble situations of heightened, institutionalized risk than disasters.

Quarantelli observes that crisis researchers have traditionally distinguished conflict situations from disasters. From the early 1950s on, there has been a consensus that disasters are generally characterized by consensual, prosocial behavior, while conflict situations are marked by some parties' interest in prolonging the disruption. There is convergence to disaster locations but avoidance or movement away from conflict, and disaster victims tend to be law-abiding and cooperative, whereas participants in conflicts are more likely to loot and obstruct medical assistance.[14]

To the nonspecialist, disasters have an accidental nature, which is related to the factor of surprise when they occur: the normal, structured, everyday aspect of some form of human life is suddenly and directly ruptured via events that initially exceed customary social and physical prediction and control. This instant, unpredicted nature of disaster—whenever and wherever it may occur—together with a historical and contemporary certainty that some disasters will occur in the near and intermediate future, renders the inevitable fact of disaster a compelling moral or ethical subject. Human well-being and harm will be at stake in ensuing disasters, and this in itself creates moral obligations to prepare for disaster and reflect on the moral principles that do or do not apply in responding to disaster.

OVERVIEW OF PARTS I AND II AND CHAPTERS

Part I addresses ethical issues raised by disaster, beginning in chapter 1 with the obligation to prepare in ways that preserve existing primary moral principles. Chapter 2 considers classic and contemporary disaster scenarios that philosophers call "lifeboat ethics." These cases raise questions concerning which moral system is best suited to disaster, consequentialism or deontology? It turns out that neither a maximization of consequences nor adherence to moral principles without exception fully and without qualification serves unpredictable life-and-death situations. The right virtues are also needed. Chapter 3 applies classic virtue ethics to disaster cases by considering which virtues are best suited to disaster. I suggest that integrity and diligence are preferable to glory-seeking bravery and ferocity.

Part II is about politics, in the sense of political theory. Morality and political theory are inextricably linked. Human beings neither construct their moral systems nor carry them out in purely individual or merely social ways. As Aristotle observed, just individuals require a just state to support their virtues. The reverse is also true—just or virtuous government requires just or virtuous citizens. In the Western social contract tradition, the justification of government itself is inherently moral. Government is understood to have been founded, and to legitimately continue in existence, because human life is better with it than without it.

Chapter 4 applies to disaster for those aspects of social contract theory deriving from John Locke's *Second Treatise of Government* that were relevant to the founding documents of the United States. Government is justified in comparison to life without government in a "state of nature." But contemporary society depends on government in ways that block return to existence in a state of nature because self-sufficient life on the land is no longer possible, and even if it were, the land itself might be destroyed. However, disasters may constitute a "second state of nature." I argue that government has an obligation, based on the justification of its origins, to prepare citizens for survival in second states of nature caused by disaster. Such preparation requires implementation through public policy.

Public policy is the subject of chapter 5. The events of 9/11, particularly the crash of American Airlines Flight 77 into the Pentagon, were followed by the creation of the Department of Homeland Security, of which the Federal Emergency Management Agency (FEMA) is now a subsidiary part. This organizational structure and post-9/11 apprehensions have resulted in a conflation of security with safety in ways that might not best serve disaster preparation and response.

Current public policy for disaster tends to issue from the perspective of officials rather than possible disaster victims. In that process, the moral importance of individual dignity may be overlooked. Chapter 6 develops a focus on disaster victims through a consideration of those with prior disadvantage, specifically African Americans after Hurricane Katrina. Other groups, such as the disabled, also experience institutional inequalities that are magnified by disaster. Because disaster preparation cannot be expected to correct these historical disadvantages and because we cannot predict which groups will suffer most in future disasters, need-based models for preparation and response are advocated.

The conclusion draws together the main claims of Parts I and II, with attention to practical and theoretical problems encountered in the development of the chapters. The result is a Code of Ethics for Disaster. Moral reflection on disaster has further implications for what counts as a disaster, and I end with a brief consideration of the global water shortage. The postscript reiterates the value of human life with reference to how life is "priced" at this time.

NOTES

1. See www.infoplease.com/world/disasters/2008.html.

2. See www.bbc.co.uk/weather/features/understanding/tsunami2.shtml.

3. The full text of Voltaire's poem can be found at http://courses.essex.ac.uk/cs/cs101/VOLT/Lisbon2.htm. Rousseau's reply as discussed below, can be found at http://faculty.gilman.edu/us/jamiespragins/Euro_Hum_2002-03/Voltaire/lisbon2.htm. Source, 7, Rousseau, Jean-Jacques. "Letter to Voltaire Regarding the Poem on the Lisbon Earthquake," August 18, 1756, Source 7 from Oeuvres completes de Voltaire, nouvelle edition, vol. 9 (Paris: Garnier, 1877), P. 470. Translated by Julius R. Ruff. (Acessed

August 2008). For discussion of the Lisbon earthquake as an event influential in European thought, see T. D. Kendrick, *The Lisbon Earthquake* (London: Methuen and Co., 1956).

4. Ibid.

5. A contemporary reflection of still-current issues raised by this episode can be found in Russell R. Dynes, "The Dialogue between Voltaire and Rousseau on the Lisbon Earthquake: The Emergence of a Social Science View," Disaster Research Center, www.udel.edu/DRC/preliminary/ pp294.pdf. accessed September 2008.

6. Both of these definitions are from www.pitt.edu/AFShome/e/p/epi2170/public/html/lecture15/sld007.htm (accessed September 2007).

7. See World Health Organization, "2007 AISA Epidemic Update/Sub-Saharan Africa," UNAIDS, March 2008, data.unaids.org/pub/Report/2008/jc1526_epibriefs_ssafrica_en.pdf.

8. Ulrick Beck, *Risk Society: Toward a New Modernity* (London: Sage, 1992), and Beck, "Risk Society Revisited: Theory Practice, and Research Programs," in *The Risk Society and Beyond: Critical Issues for Social Theory*, ed. Barbara Adam, Ulrich Beck, and Joost Van Loon (London: Sage, 2000), 211–29.

9. Gregg Easterbrook, "Road Kill: Why Are We So Worried about Terrorism When So Many More People Are Dying on Our Highways?" *LA Times*, August 5, 2006, op-ed, http://articles.latimes.com/2007/aug/05/opinion/op-easterbrook5.

10. Easterbrook, "Road Kill."

11. See W. Waut Gibbs and Christine Soares, "Preparing for a Pandemic: Are We Ready?" *Scientific American*, Special Report, November 2005. http://www.sciam.com/article.cfm?id=preparing-for-a-pandemic-2005-11 For more recent information, see www.influenza.com (accessed June 2007).

12. E. L. Quarantelli, "Epilogue: Where We Have Been and Where We Might Go: Putting the Elephant Together, Blowing Soap Bubbles, and Having Singular Insights," in *What Is a Disaster? Perspectives on the Question*, ed. E. L. Quarantelli (London: Routledge, 1998), 234–73 (description of core concepts on 234 and attempt at reconciliation of them on 273).

13. Quarantelli, "Epilogue," 236.

14. Quarantelli, "Epilogue," 238–41.

I

ETHICS

1

Disaster Planning

Is Saving the Greatest Number Best?

What persons in authority intend to do and carry out in disasters is an ethical matter because it involves human well-being. Disaster preparation occurs in normal times, and disaster response occurs immediately after a disaster or when one is imminent. Both preparation and response require plans, and both kinds of plans have ethical aspects. Is there an ethics of disaster-preparation planning distinct from an ethics of disaster-response planning?

One reason for stipulating a distinction between planning for, or in, preparation and planning for, or in, response is that the unexpected may occur, requiring unanticipated actions and rules of action. For example, there could be a plan for the orderly evacuation of a place, but in an earthquake, exit routes might be blocked, requiring the improvisation of new exit routes and evacuation methods. Perhaps the preparation plan does not require helicopter rescues, but developing circumstances do, so this is included in the response plan. A change like this does not entail a change in ethical principles, provided the intention that everyone be safely evacuated is present in both plans. One way to avoid apparent contradictions between preparation and response plans is to make the preparation plans sufficiently general. For example, safe evacuation of all occupants is stated as a primary goal in the preparation plan, and several exit routes are specified beforehand, but the choice of exit route is left open, to be determined by actual circumstances.

There may be a different kind of change, however, whereby a rule involving human well-being is different in the preparation and response plans. Suppose it is known beforehand that preparation will be inadequate, and plans are made to save a limited number. Can such a response plan be ethically justified, or is it unethical? Perhaps we can begin to answer this question by considering how crises other than contemporary disasters have been morally assessed.

MEDICAL TRIAGE IN WAR

The unexpected and sudden harms incurred in war have been systematically addressed with principles and practices of triage since the Napoleonic era. The reality of mass casualties and officials' imperative to deal with them still evoke military medical history in contemporary discussions of disaster. Thus, Gerald Winslow begins *Triage and Justice* with a fairly standard definition of triage that links civilian disaster with war:

> *Triage.* . . . The medical screening of patients to determine their priority for treatment, the separation of a large number of casualties, in military or civilian disaster medical care, into three groups: those who cannot be expected to survive even with treatment, those who will recover without treatment, and the priority group of those who need treatment in order to survive.[1]

In a now-classic 1992 essay, "Triage and Equality," Robert Baker and Martin Strosberg distinguish between two kinds of triage deriving from modern wars, the egalitarian model and the utilitarian, or efficiency, model.[2] Baron Dominique Jean Larrey, Napoleon's surgeon general, developed the egalitarian model of triage. Larrey based his system of sorting and transporting the wounded on the principle that "those who are dangerously wounded must be tended first, entirely without regard to rank or distinction."[3] Larrey's objective was not the efficient utilitarian goal of restoring the wounded for the sake of the war objective but the egalitarian utilitarian goal of treating the most gravely wounded, who would receive the greatest benefit from immediate care and die without it. Baker and Strosberg explain how Larrey's model of "methodical succor" allocates scare resources to maximize results without detriment to anyone's interests: the gravely wounded are saved; the lightly wounded may be saved in the future should they be seriously wounded, and they are not harmed by waiting for treatment in the present; the moribund are not harmed because they would not benefit from treatment. Baker and Strosberg further note that "methodical succor" is common practice in contemporary emergency and intensive medical care.[4]

Baker and Strosberg pinpoint how, in military terms, the efficiency model of medical triage departs from the egalitarian model. The efficiency model seeks to maximize the results of medical triage in terms of the military requirement that at any given time there must be as many physically able soldiers as possible. According to J. Tristram Engelhardt and Albert Jonsen's reprisal of Raul Ramsey, "Speedy restoration of the fighting function is the objective. *The more difficult cases wait, regardless of the seriousness of their need.*" In his memoir, Dr. Henry Beecher recorded a famous application of this principle in the distribution of penicillin in North Africa during World War II. Instead of dispensing the drug to soldiers with broken bones incurred during battle, it was given to those infected with venereal disease from patronizing brothels. The second group could be more quickly returned to the front, although the moral objection was considered to be significant.[5]

Michael Gross draws an even sharper contrast between egalitarian and efficient utilitarian triage in war. According to the First and Second 1949 Geneva Conventions, "Only urgent medical reasons will authorize priority in the order of treatment to be administered" (Geneva Convention I, II, 1949, Art. 12, para. 3). Moreover, the 1977 Geneva Protocols extend this principle to include enemy wounded (Protocol I, 1977b, Art. 10, para. 453). However, the U.S. Department of Defense in 1988 directed that the goal of medical triage was the "maximum number of salvageable soldiers," which contradicts both the order of, and preferred subjects for, treatment specified by the Geneva Protocols.[6] NATO's directives are also based on salvage. Military protocols based on maximizing salvage are thus clearly opposed to egalitarian principles of triage.

Two important points emerge from this discussion of war triage as it relates to disaster. First, medical triage in war occurs under special pressures, when little can be done to augment preparation. Scarcity of supplies, time, and resources is intractable, so the primary ethical concerns are restricted to the best response. Furthermore, it is a legitimate expectation that some will be maimed or die. By contrast, it is in principle possible to prepare for disaster, so the occurrence of casualties need not be accepted beforehand. Second, observers agree that over time in democratic societies, a conflict between public ideals of fairness, or egalitarianism, and practitioners' goals of efficiency will be resolved in favor of fairness, even under the pressures of war. If egalitarianism is preferred to efficiency as a model for war triage, there should be a lesson here concerning relevant moral principles for disaster triage. However, while disaster does not have the same urgency of outcome as war (because the lives of others beyond those fighting in the war may be at stake), disaster can be even more unpredictable and disorganized than war, especially when disasters that lack preparation are compared to military events.

Robert Veatch suggests that the preference of egalitarian measures over efficiency for allocating transplanted organs preserves ideals of justice in ways that are relevant to triage plans in mass disaster. Following the deliberations of the Ethics Committee of the United Network for Organ Sharing, Veatch proposes that there should at least be broad discussion of the egalitarian

versus efficiency models.[7] Triage of scarce medical resources in normal life
may furnish comparative examples between war and disaster. Shared moral
ideals not only have the best chance of being realized in normal life but are
likely to come out of normal life. Furthermore, for disaster casualties,
unlike war, there is no higher or further purpose beyond saving the lives of
immediate victims (i.e., no civilian population that is being kept safe as
casualties occur).

To understand the public preference for fairness over efficiency, we need
to remember that, in the long run, peace and normal life are eventually restored, allowing the values of the civilian public to reassert themselves.
Contemporary disasters affect civilians in the midst of their ordinary lives.
For that reason alone, normal ethical perspectives would be expected to inform acceptable disaster preparation. Also, disaster preparation itself would
thereby be expected to bear more resemblance to normal forms of planning
than to planning how to respond efficiently with scarce resources in war because only the lives and well-being of those involved in the disaster—as
compared to soldiers, who play a protective role—are directly affected.

ETHICS OF PLANNING IN ORDINARY LIFE

Once we have the structure of ordinary planning in mind and some clear
intuitions about how planning is an ethical matter, it may be possible to answer the question of whether disaster-response plans can have different
guiding ethical principles than disaster-preparation plans. In normal, more
or less predictable, everyday life, there is no distinction between preparation
or plans/principles *for* action and application or plans/principles *of* action.
The plans of action are usually straightforward executions of the plans for
action, so application mirrors preparation. Most, if not all, professional activities, construction projects, and items manufactured for human consumption begin with plans, blueprints, or lists of ingredients, which have to
be approved by government or administrative authorities before action can
legally be taken. Building codes, for example, require that architectural, en-
vironmental-impact, and safety measures be detailed in plans, which must
be approved before construction can begin. It is assumed that construction
will then take place according to the approved plans, and to make sure that
it does, different stages of construction are inspected by officials who report
to the agencies that approved the plans. The approved ingredients listed on
containers of medication and food are supposed (i.e., both required and assumed) to be present in the proportions listed within the containers. Professions governed by codes of ethics approved by their members function
on the assumption that these codes will not be violated in practice. When

they are violated, practitioners may be guilty of malpractice, incurring criminal, as well as civil and professional, penalties.

In general, human commercial and professional life takes place according to prior plans that have been approved to safeguard against danger and fraud. The nature of the approved plans, the match between approved plans and consequent action and production, and the quality of the products and action are all subject to ethical principles, which are largely implicit. Moreover, the relevant information about plans and ingredients is accessible to those who will be affected by them. This openness of relevant information is based on the assumption that people have a right to know about products and services insofar as they are affected by them. It goes without saying that consumers, buyers, patients, and clients should not be harmed by professional services and business products and that they should not be deceived about what they are getting. When it is known beforehand that they may be harmed by a product (e.g., cigarettes) or an activity (e.g., sky diving), it is considered appropriate that the end consumer or user assume some of the risk involved so that sellers or service providers are not fully liable for any resulting harm.

The widespread acceptance of the Principle of No Harm (PNH) gives rise to legal and financial liability when harm has occurred. When professionals, manufacturers, business people, and sellers submit appropriate plans that are in due course approved, part of the motivation for the approval process is the avoidance of liability or responsibility for harm. The other part of the approval process implicitly rests on the moral importance of PNH itself, although even that is not the complete moral picture. At the base of avoiding harm for both legal and moral reasons is the positive value of human well-being. According to the general *Principle of Well-Being* (PWB), products and services should contribute to the well-being of end users and consumers. It is, moreover, understood that well-being is loosely construed to include pleasure and entertainment, as well as prosperity, convenience, and health. (For instance, if fast food and sugar-laden snacks did not taste good, so that their nutritional deficits were the whole truth about them, their desirability would plummet.)

Not only is the general presumption that goods and services promote human well-being a standard for what is produced and performed, but it motivates planning itself and makes prudence a virtue. The carpenter who measures twice and cuts once not only makes good bookshelves but is a good carpenter. Good planning not only makes the practitioner a good practitioner but also reflects positively on her moral character. As a result, planning is both morally and practically required for all important endeavors, and it is itself subject to moral scrutiny, apart from its results. Planning is a required duty of trustees, stewards, and guardians. Planning is a general responsibility of every adult as an integral part of caring for oneself and for others to and for whom we have prior obligations.

ETHICS OF DISASTER PLANNING

In normal life, we can count on work more or less going according to plan, whereas in disasters, our best plans may not be applicable. That we do not know beforehand which parts of our plans for disaster will fail to be applicable itself puts restrictions on the whole dimension of planning for disaster. First, insofar as planning is part of preparation, it has to occur before a disaster is present or imminent; if not done beforehand, it is likely to be influenced by immediate pressures that could cloud moral judgment. Disaster planning as part of preparation needs to be unbiased, and so long as there is assumed to be time, there is no reason to compromise on what ought to be done because preparation occurs in normal times. Second, disaster-preparation planning has to be general, but not so general as to be morally or factually vacuous. Third, disaster planning ought to express our best moral principles and not go against them, but it must also be practical, or possible, to execute. And fourth, we are obligated to plan optimistically in the sense that we ought not to make plans that we know will violate existing moral principles or do not believe will achieve desired goals. That is, optimistic planning is based on the assumption that it is possible to plan well.

The known fact of contingencies, without knowing precisely what those contingencies will be, entails that disaster preparation is not the same thing as disaster rehearsal. No matter how many mock disasters are staged according to prior plans, the real disaster will never mirror any one of them. Disaster-preparation planning is more like training for a marathon than training for a high-jump competition or a sprinting event. Marathon runners do not practice by running the full course of twenty-six miles; rather, they get into shape by running shorter distances and building up their endurance with cross-training. If they have prepared successfully, then they are in optimal condition to run the marathon over its predetermined course and length, assuming a range of weather conditions, predicted or not. This is normal marathon preparation.

But imagine preparing for a mystery marathon on undisclosed terrain, of an unspecified length, which could begin at any time. There would be many different ways to prepare for those uncertainties, and participants would be in varied stages of preparation when the start of the mystery marathon was announced. Rehearsal would be even more clearly out of the question than in the case of the normal marathon. Of course, one need not participate in either a normal or a mystery marathon, and human well-being is not at stake (beyond optional choices), so it is not necessary, much less morally required, to prepare for one. In contrast, we do not have a choice about whether a disaster will occur where we happen to be, or when, and our responsibilities to ourselves and others require that we do prepare.

To summarize, disaster preparation is an ethical matter, and it is mandatory. The planning component of this preparation must be general enough to allow for unforeseen contingences and must take place in normal times, before a disaster occurs or is imminent. Disaster plans must be consistent with normal planning principles of not intending harm and positively preserving human well-being. Furthermore, the disaster plan, as part of preparation, is distinct from both the action in any particular response and the principles governing such action. Finally, in an open, democratic society, the general disaster plan(s) should be public information because the public will be affected. It follows from this that if the plans do not conform to PNH or PWB, they should be revised; if they cannot be revised, there should be extensive public discussion about which harms are unavoidable.

CURRENT AVIAN FLU PANDEMIC PLANNING AND WIDER ETHICAL IMPLICATIONS

Although disaster planning is not a new human enterprise—we are a relatively prudent species—planning for specific probable disasters may entail new projects for the policy analysts and ethicists called upon to consider them as new dangers. It is perhaps understandable that these experts, under a present sense of urgency, direct their planning efforts to specific contingencies, which is to say that they construct plans for response. However, the *absence* of general preparation plans, deliberately constructed in what are assumed to be normal times and explicitly based on PNH and PWB, is a striking feature of much contemporary disaster literature. To the extent that specific emergency-response plans are presented as ethically sound emergency response plans, a crucial part of the deliberative process has been left out, especially when those response plans adopt guidelines pertaining to human well-being that would not be accepted either in disaster-preparation plans crafted by practitioners, or by the public if it were informed about them.

There are at least three big obstacles for an adequate response to an Avian Flu pandemic, based on what is now known about the disease and existing medical infrastructure. First, even if enough flu vaccine could be produced to inoculate half or more of the population against Avian Flu, it is very difficult to predict the specific strain(s) of Avian Flu that will hit, far enough in advance to make sufficient vaccine, and any strain that does hit could mutate in unpredictable ways.[8] This is the problem of a changing viral target. The second obstacle to an adequate Avian Flu pandemic response at this time is that it takes months to develop an effective vaccine once the target virus has been identified. Thus, the epidemic would be well underway before the right vaccine was available. Both the changing target and the time frame required to grow the vaccine are problems with prevention, and there is no easy solution to them at present. The third big obstacle to an adequate response is that there are limited resources in terms of numbers of hospital beds, ventilators, and antiviral medications. As a result, it is now unlikely to be possible to treat everyone who becomes ill with the virus.[9]

At present, there seems to be a model for Avian Flu response plans, which purports to delineate the allocation of scare resources in a principled way. The model is evident in ethical guidelines submitted in 2007 by the Ethics Subcommittee of the Advisory Committee to the Director of the U.S. Centers for Disease Control and Prevention,[10] a 2006 report of the University of Toronto Joint Centre for Bioethics Pandemic Influenza Working Group,[11] and more specific articles about scarce triage in conditions of inadequate resources.[12] The guidelines specify that government officials need to control contagion by limiting normal institutional gatherings (e.g., school attendance) and social contact at commercial and entertainment venues; provisions for quarantine are also deemed necessary. Normal emergency triage is invoked, meaning that those who are likely to benefit from immediate medical attention should receive treatment first, deferring treatment of moribund cases and those with minor complaints. Most readers and members of the public would find all of the foregoing components of the current response plan model well in accord with common sense, as well as morally acceptable.

However, two further aspects of the current model for Avian Flu response do require closer moral scrutiny because they depart from egalitarian principles taken for granted in normal life. The first is the stipulation that priority of immunization and treatment be given to health care professionals and providers of vital public services and utilities. The second involves a "triage of triage," whereby not everyone who would benefit from immediate medical attention in a first-order triage will get it owing to different levels of scarcity. Some writers suggest that "remaining life years," "preexisting medical conditions," and vaguer measures of "human worth" be assigned numerical "ranks" in order to determine whether treatment will be given to specific individuals. In an Avian Flu pandemic, ventilators are likely to be the most desired scarce resource, and it has been suggested that patients already on ventilators for nonflu conditions or those with the flu who are not responding as well as anticipated be removed from them so that the ventilators can be reassigned.[13]

It should further be noted that the current versions of Avian Flu pandemic response plans all stipulate that open public discussion of the plans is necessary. While the plans are presently being discussed by emergency personnel on many local levels throughout the United States,[14] as of December 2008, there appears to have been no widespread public promulgation of the strategy of triage or identification of preferred recipients of treatment. In semiprivate discussion among health care professionals, it may seem as though, in a pandemic, the patient is no longer the individual human being but the community.[15] From this perspective, measures that would not be acceptable for individual care but which seem to insure the survival of "the community" appear to be more ethically acceptable. (More will be said about this "community" at the end of the following section.)

PREPARATION VERSUS RESPONSE PLANNING

A response plan is not the same as a plan for preparation. To prepare means "to become ready." Becoming ready for a pandemic has an element of engagement consisting of being able and willing to act, as well as an element of having what it takes for a successful outcome. In a war, a small group of soldiers might be able and willing to engage an enemy, believing in advance that most of them will die and that the enemy will not be defeated. They may have prepared themselves psychically for the engagement, but this does not mean that they are materially prepared to defeat the enemy. An army might be prepared for the same enemy so that its response has the same psychic component as the small group, but its greater numbers and more extensive weaponry would constitute the kind of preparation likely to yield a successful outcome.

For any probable disaster, preparation requires both the material and the active response capabilities that will make a successful outcome likely. In an Avian Flu pandemic, this would require sufficient immunization materials, antiviral medications, and trained personnel so that those who would receive medical treatment for emergencies in normal times would receive it in the pandemic. The present problem is with sufficient material and skilled medical personnel—to the point where experts have said that the world is no better prepared for a current pandemic than it was almost a century ago, when forty million died in the Spanish Flu pandemic![16] But we could be prepared if we had sufficient material and trained personnel. A preparation plan would describe exactly what was needed for different degrees of epidemic severity: how many immunization units, which and how many antiviral doses, how many hospital beds, and how many ventilators, plus the amount of personnel and training required to deploy these resources successfully. In other words, a preparation plan could restructure the conditions of response so that adequate response could be envisioned beforehand, as not violating the ethical principles of normal life, for the reason that resources will be scarce.

The difference in ethical principle between response and preparation plans (that may not yet even exist) is one between Save the Greatest Number (SGN) and Save All Who Can Be Saved (SALL). SGN is the operating principle behind many current disaster-response plans in the United States, where it is also frequently invoked in volunteer efforts, such as Community Emergency Response Team (CERT) training.[17] However, SGN is an ethical principle that cannot be accepted without qualification. It appears to derive from the philosophical ethical tradition of utilitarianism and consequentialism, although it is a (possibly dangerous) simplification of the principles of that tradition. SALL captures a general moral consensus of Western democratic societies.

SGN is morally limited because the greatest number who can be saved depends on the context in question. If a bridge is well maintained against collapse, and the community has an adequate emergency-response plan, then everyone who can be saved will have been saved if the bridge never collapses—or if it does collapse, and there is a successful rescue. Both are examples of SALL. But suppose that the bridge is not maintained, it collapses, and a number of people are crushed. The rescue effort may apply SGN to the survivors, but lost forever are those who would not have been crushed had the bridge been well maintained. If there has been inadequate preparation for the rescue, the application of SGN will result in even fewer "saves." Thus, although SGN can always be fulfilled in an immediate situation, there may still be losses that could have been prevented. SGN is therefore a limited, because it is a relative, utilitarian principle. SALL is more comprehensive and more stable for any given disaster because it requires that preparation and prevention, as well as response, be considered. If the bridge is adequately maintained and does not collapse, or if it collapses and there is a well-prepared rescue response, then everyone who can be saved, will be saved. The difference between SGN and SALL, which are both utilitarian principles, is that SALL takes both preparation and response into account, whereas SGN is focused on response.

Preparation is not response. By the time we must respond or are thinking about how to respond, the time to prepare will have passed. Preparation, unlike response, by its nature takes place in normal times, without the pressures of having to act immediately. It is during preparation in normal times—that is, normal in contrast to the disaster being prepared for—that we are obligated to work out the moral principles that will guide specific plans of response. This includes examining our existing moral principles and applying them to future stages of preparation itself. That is, our existing moral principles dictate not only how we intend to respond but what further preparation is necessary.[18]

There is nothing mysterious about what "our" existing moral (or ethical) principles are because they are based on values that, in the Western tradition at least, are the result of millennia of religious and humanistic study and practice. Moreover, these principles and values are immediately recognizable as right to those who minimally share the heritage of a democratic society. Thus,

1. Human life has intrinsic worth.
2. Everyone's life is equally valuable.
3. Everyone has the same right to freedom from harm by others.
4. Everyone is entitled to protection from harm by nonhuman forces.

Democratic government is obligated, and assumed, to support principles 1 to 4, which are general *social* principles. These principles become ethical rules for individuals in the following ways:

A. We are obligated to care for ourselves and our dependents.
B. We are obligated not to harm one another.
C. We are obligated to care for strangers when it doesn't harm us to do so.

Both lists are incomplete and might be expressed differently, but together they capture the common morality of peaceful, normal life in democratic societies.[19] They should therefore serve as ethical guidelines when the physical order and resources that support normal life are interrupted, impaired, or destroyed by disaster, and they or something like them, should guide preparation for disaster.[20]

The common ethical values of peaceful life ought to be recognized in disaster planning as part of that preparation for disaster, which is undertaken in normal times. In disasters themselves, or in the formulation of response plans, these values may function as ideals. To the extent that a specific response plan falls short of such ideals, it fails to be moral or ethical. An ethical response plan requires adherence to common ethical principles. To call a response plan "ethical," it is not sufficient, as the current trend suggests, simply to append the label "ethical" to an issue involving human well-being and to recommend that those carrying out the response not be held legally liable for the results of actions that would not be considered ethical in normal times.

It is not ethics that are relative to circumstances, but the goodness or badness of circumstances that are relative to expectations. In this sense, bad circumstances are not an excuse for bad ethics. In many parts of the world, including some areas of the United States, large numbers of people live amid great physical danger without the amenities taken for granted by those who are, by comparison, privileged. We do not thereby indemnify those who are disadvantaged from ordinary ethical obligations, even though the trauma and deprivations they suffer may be equal to or worse than what we who are privileged would experience in a disaster. From the perspective of a life that is normally relatively privileged, difficult and dangerous circumstances that exist elsewhere, while privileged normal life unfolds "here," are not considered a moral holiday for those experiencing the difficulty and danger. Therefore, those who normally live relatively privileged lives ought not to give themselves a moral holiday when they plan how to respond to what would be a disaster for them. If we think that it is wrong for strong governments in poor societies to enforce life-and-death disparities in medical treatment, how can it be right for us to enforce such disparities during our disasters? We call "unjust" those societies that allow infants, the elderly, and the disabled to die of treatable diseases, while medical treatment is available to a selected few. How, then, can we call such policies "ethical" when they are incorporated into disaster-response plans for our own society?

Disaster preparation should take place in normal times under the same moral guidelines that we customarily accept. As indicated in the Avian Flu pandemic examples, experts have left out the entire stage of planning as part of preparation and gone straight to the kind of response planning that could be appropriate after the disaster has struck or is imminent, in a situation of limited resources or inadequate preparation. But since any pandemic will occur in waves over a period of months, it is not clear what motivates this rush. Nevertheless, in general, our best preparation at any given stage may be inadequate in the event of a sudden and unexpected catastrophe.

The foregoing ethical analysis posits that we should not plan in advance how to allocate scare resources because we should not accept such scarcity while there is time to augment resources or otherwise adequately prepare. Yet, common sense or prudence might suggest that we should engage in that exercise of scarce-resource allocation as part of our preparation for events that cannot be precisely predicted or rehearsed. So, this brings us back to the question of how scarce resources ought to be allocated, back to the question of how to triage triage itself. The philosopher John Rawls is helpful here. In his famous thought experiment on justice, Rawls advocates that the planners of a just society with scarce resources deliberate behind a "veil of ignorance" concerning their own interests. The deliberators are not to know whether they themselves are rich or poor, young or old, or members of dominant or disadvantaged racial and ethnic groups.[21] Of course, in reality, people cannot easily forget their own interests in this way, and history yields few examples of such "ignorant" deliberation having been undertaken by even the most altruistic of government or institutional framers. Rawls's point, however, is that democratic political theorists ought to examine and critique basic government structures and institutions against the standard of the thought experiment of the veil of ignorance, because that "original position" (in Rawls's terminology) will guarantee fairness. Fairness for Rawls is his conception or application of justice, whereby justice is the primary virtue of any society. Can we apply this idea of a "veil of ignorance" toward a fair allocation of scarce resources in a disaster? Yes, because while Rawls had the basic structures of society in mind, rather than specific policies, his "model" of the veil can be applied to specific policies.

In the present case of framing a response plan to an Avian Flu pandemic, the planners ought not to know if they are themselves elderly, already ill, disabled, or young and healthy. Neither should they know whether they are poets, kindergarten teachers, clergy, cops, or the government officials, public-policy experts, medical personnel, and commissioned ethicists *who they already are*. The aim is to approximate a condition in which members of groups likely to get preferred allocations of scarce resources are not the ones crafting response plans. This is not to say that such individuals are not fine human beings of high moral principles; it is merely to ensure a structure of fairness. It is interesting to note that Winslow, who applies Rawlsian principles of deliberation and justice to triage, considers it acceptable in disaster to give priority in the allocation of scarce medical resources to medical personnel, police, and firemen. However, Winslow's justification is not the straightforward utilitarian calculation that this will save more lives in the long run but the presumption that those "behind the veil," who did not know their occupations, would choose such an allocation. According to Winslow's Rawlsian reasoning, they would choose it because it would promote greater equality of access to treatment, particularly for those who are most in need of it. (That is, according to a Rawlsian "difference principle," unequal distribution is justified if those worse off benefit from it.[22])

The distinction between a direct utilitarian allocation of scarce resources and a utilitarian allocation that is voluntary is exactly the distinction Baker and Strosberg draw between egalitarian and efficiency utilitarianism. That is, egalitarianism may have utilitarian goals, but it must be voluntary, whereas efficiency measures to maximize utilitarian goals need not be voluntary, or chosen by all who participate and are affected.[23]

One way to practically ensure fairness about who gets to decide what the response plan should be, given scarce resources, would be to enable the broad public discussion of how scarce resources ought to be allocated. Such public discussion is in fact a stated requirement of the response plan model now widely accepted, although it has not yet occurred either in "town meeting" formats in the United States or through broad media promulgation of the model itself. In a democratic society, it is an empirical question how those who will now not likely get either immunization or antiviral treatment or their advocates would "vote" regarding the allocation of these scarce resources. And, it would seem to be ethically imperative to ask the public, as a matter of principled, democratic public policy. Would most people prefer that vital public service personnel receive priority in the allocation of scarce resources in a disaster? And if so, what kinds of safe-guards would be appropriate to make sure that those who received priority treatment did continue their rescue efforts? Notice that if the public does prefer priority treatment for medical and public service personnel, this is-sue will have been moved to preparation planning in a principled way.

Broad public discussion of the allocation of limited resources in emer-gencies should be a vital component of disaster preparation in a democratic society, a component thus far overlooked. The outcome may be no change in the recommended resource-allocation hierarchies in present response plans. It is also possible that strong public objection by those unlikely to re-ceive treatment and/or by their advocates could motivate and invigorate the part of preparation that would result in adequate supplies of vaccination and antiviral materials for an Avian Flu pandemic. Perhaps this view is overly optimistic about the degree of the public's interest in its own welfare. Perhaps the public at this time is only capable of reacting when policies in effect in a pandemic or other disaster are directly experienced as unethical. Again, this is an empirical question that can only be answered through the kind of communication that is a requirement of adequate preparation.

Broad communication during preparation would give a literal meaning to the use of the term *community* in mass triage response plans. The com-munity would consist of participating discussants, including advocates for those who do not speak. This community of discourse would constitute and represent all those likely to be affected by a disaster. The idea that "the com-munity is the patient" is a standing heuristic in public medicine during nor-mal times. But during normal times, this is an *abstract* heuristic idea, and the individual remains the patient in practice. The normal use of the phrase "treating the community" directs attention to social issues and measures that will enhance individual health and well-being. However, it is not clear what constitutes "the community" during an event with mass casualties, in contexts where concern is expressed for "saving the community." Is the community the neighborhood, town, city, county, or state? Does the com-munity include the moral values taken for granted in normal times? Can the community be saved if much of its material infrastructure is destroyed? When "save the community" is another way of saying "save the greatest number of survivors in the community," it is difficult to see how anything more than a rhetorical purpose is served, along the lines of, "Communities are good. This plan saves the community. Therefore this plan is good."

SAVING THE GREATEST NUMBER

At present in emergency preparation, the operating moral rule for rescue professionals—which, though not quite a law, is in most cases accepted as not in violation of law and therefore has the protection of law after the fact—is *Save the Greatest Number* (SGN). It's not known beforehand what SGN may entail in any given case because what the greatest number is will depend on time constraints, hazards to rescue operations, and limits in personnel and material resources. In emergency medical terms, SGN of course translates into "triage." Sort the injured into those who are likely to die from mortal injuries, those who have minor injuries, and those who require quick medical attention but are likely to survive if they get it. The third group is treated first. This is the emergency protocol in situations of normal emergencies, such as vehicular accidents.[24]

But, as noted, mass casualties may evoke another kind of triage, in response to limited resources, when it is impossible to treat all those who are likely to survive if they get quick medical attention.[25] When SGN is applied to exclude from treatment the elderly, the already ill, those lacking good long-term prognoses, or those deemed less worthy of treatment, SGN has become SGN Who ___ (SGNW), where the blank is filled in by the predetermined characteristics of patients who will receive treatment. Moreover, the dynamic nature of catastrophes and unpredicted damage may result in greater resource scarcity, so that the blank in SGNW will have to be filled in or revised in an immediate situation, and perhaps revised again as that situation changes.[26]

There are two moral problems with SGNW. First, it puts arbitrary power over life and death in the hands of individuals in ways that are not transparent to the public, either before or after the fact. While such individuals may have the legitimacy of official administrative or medical positions in disaster situations, they are not otherwise certified or, so far as the public knows, morally qualified to hold and execute such power. More to the point, it is by no means answerable what such "moral qualification" could be. Second, the SGNW model or formula accepts a limitation of resources before the fact, when there may still be time to ensure that there are enough resources through more extended preparation. The fact that SGN is in accord with common sense and ordinary prudence gives it an appearance of moral legitimacy. And the justification for filling in the blank in "Who ___ " with medical or law enforcement personnel, is that the greatest number will indeed be saved if they have priority in treatment. Furthermore, SGNW need not preclude saving those who do not match the required description; it only mandates giving those who do match it priority. However, there is much left unanswered by SGNW. Is it possible to save all who are given priority? Would members of the public accept SGNW if they knew beforehand that they would not be given priority? What should be done with the loved ones of those who are given priority, and how will that further affect SGN?

Ideally, in a disaster, everyone who can be saved after a catastrophic event is in fact saved: *Save All Who Can Be Saved* (SALL). And if we cannot envision

SALL in normal times while there is still time to prepare, then we have not fulfilled our obligation to plan for disasters. We are already familiar with SALL because it is the rule for normal emergency preparation. For example, in July 2006, after a woman was killed by a collapsed panel in Boston's "Big Dig" tunnel, the governor of Massachusetts took over the investigation of structural problems with the tunnel, and the tunnel was closed pending complete investigation and repair.[27] The reasoning here could not have been SGN, which would have resulted in triage after another accident.[28] Instead, the reasoning was (i.e., seems to have been) SALL. Shutting down the tunnel for a complete inspection and repairs will have saved everyone who could be saved from future collapses beforehand—or at least that would be the goal.

A similar preventative principle seems to be at work in efforts to build vehicles capable of withstanding collisions and requiring not only that they contain passenger restraints but that passengers use them. With the Big Dig, however, the intention was to prevent future accidents from a specific cause by eliminating that cause (faulty construction). This is probably an example of disaster prevention (although if the tunnel were refortified against external stresses, it would be disaster mitigation). In the design and manufacture of vehicles, the intent is to minimize the damage from collisions, which is, strictly speaking, *disaster mitigation*.[29] Thus, some disaster preparation involves prevention of causes (such as efforts to apprehend terrorists before they carry out acts of terror), whereas other forms of disaster preparation involve having an effective response after the disaster has occurred. Clearly, both forms of preparation are important. If we are not adequately prepared, we will be stuck with SGN after a catastrophe, and if we accept inadequate preparation beforehand, we will morally compromise ourselves with SGNW.

But what happens if SALL is applied with adequate prior preparation, a disaster occurs, and there are still not enough resources to save everyone who can be saved? Is it then morally justified to operate under SGNW? Unless there has been broad public discussion about what characteristics should be used to fill in the blank, the answer is no. In the absence of principled consensus, no one has the right to "play God." So, what should be done by those who have to decide whom to save in situations where everyone who could be saved, given adequate resources, cannot be saved as a result of inadequate resources? It seems as though the only fair way to make such decisions would be randomly, or on a first-come, first-serve basis. Indeed, during a pandemic, all ill patients will not present themselves for treatment at the same time. And during rescue efforts in other disasters, survivors will either present themselves for treatment, or rescuers will find them and treat them as they find them. When large numbers of survivors needing treatment are present at once, it is difficult to imagine forms of selection that go beyond normal emergency triage. The fact of limited resources cannot give some people arbitrary power over the life and death of others. The fact of limited resources in situations where people suffer through no fault of their own only puts both aid providers and sufferers in a very bad, insecure position. We are left with Fairly Save All Who Can Be Saved, with the Best Preparation (FSALLBP).

How are we to determine "the best preparation," given competing needs for resources? Do we, for example, choose more health care for normal times or more supplies for a possible pandemic? In a democracy, the answer to this question needs to be decided by open discussion and public opinion. Ideally, the best preparation will be enough preparation to avoid using scarce resources as a justification for planning responses that violate the broad ethical principles of normal times. References to scarce resources as a justification for current triage models that fall short of fairly saving all who can be saved miss the relevant moral issue here. It is morally right to save all who can be saved. It may be that we cannot afford to do that as part of adequate preparation. This is a very unfortunate situation. But financial constraints are not grounds for revising our fundamental moral principles. Moral principles are not luxuries that can be cut out of budgets when living up to them requires harsh reallocations and inconvenient sacrifices. It is a mainstay of ethical reasoning that "ought implies can." To say that we ought to do something assumes that it is in our power to do it. Thus far, no body of evidence, scholarly or otherwise, attests to "our" inability as a society to prepare for predictable disasters adequately.

To conclude, we are morally obligated to plan for disaster because it affects human life and well-being. Because contemporary disasters affect the public, such planning should be public in democracies and should not violate the basic ethical principles of normal times. Current Avian Flu pandemic planning is restricted to a response model based on scarce resources, or inadequate preparation, which gives priority to some lives over others. Rather than this model of SGN, the public would be more ethically served by a model of SALL, which is based on adequate preparation. And where events exceed adequate preparation, scarce resources should be allocated fairly.

NOTES

1. Gerald R. Winslow, *Triage and Justice* (Berkeley: University of California Press, 1982), 1.

2. Robert Baker and Martin Strosberg, "Triage and Equality: An Historical Reassessment of Utilitarian Analyses of Triage," *Kennedy Institute of Ethics Journal* 2, no. 2 (1992): 103–23.

3. Baker and Strosberg, "Triage and Equality," 110, from Dominique Jean Larrey, "Surgical Memoirs of the Campaign in Russia," trans. J. Mercer (Philadelphia: Cowey

and Lea, 1882), 109. However, the situation was not as clear-cut as Beecher's account implies because it was not known at the time whether penicillin would be effective in the treatment of war wounds. See Michael L. Gross, *Bioethics and Armed Conflict: Moral Dilemmas of Medicine and War* (Cambridge, MA: MIT Press, 2006).

4. Baker and Strosberg, "Triage and Equality," 111–14.

5. Baker and Strosberg, "Triage and Equality," 103–4.

6. Gross, "Bioethics and Armed Conflict," 137–41.

7. Robert M. Veatch, "Disaster Preparedness and Triage," *Mount Sinai Journal of Medicine* 72, no. 4 (July 2005): 236–41.

8. See W. Waut Gibbs and Christine Soares, "Preparing for a Pandemic: Are We Ready?" *Scientific American*, Special Report, November 2005 http://www.sciam.com/article.cfm?id=preparing-for-a-pandemic-2005-11. For more recent information, see also www.influenza.com.

9. This is a working assumption in all current Avian Flu response plans. See note 18 for references to individual state plans in the United States.

10. Kathy Kinlaw and Robert Levine, "Ethical Guidelines in Pandemic Influenza—Recommendations of the Ethics Subcommittee of the Advisory Committee to the Director," Centers for Disease Control and Prevention, February 15, 2007, www.cdc.gov/od/science/phec/panFlu_Ethic_Guidelines.pdf.

11. University of Toronto Joint Centre for Bioethics Pandemic Influenza Working Group, "Stand on Guard for Thee: Ethical Considerations in Preparedness Planning for Pandemic Influenza," University of Toronto Joint Centre for Bioethics, November 2005, www.utoronto.ca/jcb/home/documents/pandemic.pdf.

12. See, for example, L. Gostin, "Medical Countermeasures for Pandemic Influenza: Ethics and the Law," *JAMA* 295 (2006): 554–56; J. Hick and D. O'Laughlin, "Concept of Operations for Triage of Mechanical Ventilation in an Epidemic," *Academic Emergency Medicine* 13 (2006): 223–29.

13. See, for instance, Hick and O'Laughlin, "Concept of Operations."

14. In May 2006 and 2007, I attended community ethics discussions held by the Lane County Medical Association Emergency Medicine Task Force in Eugene, Oregon. Current resources in the literature on mass triage were referenced, and issues of scarce-resource allocation, immediate decisions, and liability on the part of medical personnel were discussed.

15. The term *altered standards* has not been defined but is generally assumed to mean a shift to providing care and allocating scarce equipment, supplies, and personnel in a way that saves the greatest number of lives in contrast to the traditional focus on saving individuals. For example, it could mean applying principles of field triage. See Agency for Healthcare Research and Quality (AHRQ), U.S. Department of Health and Human Services (540 Gaither Road, Rockville, MD 20850, www.ahrq.gov), "Altered Standards of Care in Mass Casualty Event," Contract No. 290-04-0010, prepared by Health Systems Research, Inc. AHRQ Publication No. 05-0043 (April 2005), www.ahrq.gov/research/altstand/altstand.pdf (accessed June 2007). Quote is from p. 10.

16. For instance, given the shortage of mechanical ventilators, family members may be called upon to provide manual ventilation as they were in 1918 (see note 8).

17. "First, present citizens the facts about what to expect following a major disaster in terms of immediate services. Second, give the message about their responsi-

bility for mitigation and preparedness. Third, train them in needed life saving skills with emphasis on decision making skills, rescuer safety, and doing the greatest good for the greatest number." See CERT at www.citizencorps.gov/cert.

18. See James C. Thomas, Nabarun Dasgupta, and Amanda Martinot, "Ethics in a Pandemic: A Survey of the State Pandemic Influenza Plans," *American Journal of Public Health* 97, no. S1 (2007): S26–S31. The authors note that in November 2005, following World Health Organization recommendations, the U.S. president's Homeland Security Council published a national strategy for a pandemic influenza plan in which the main responsibilities for planning and responding lie with state and local governments. Many of the resulting state plans pay little specific attention to ethical issues or the need for ethical deliberations. Thomas, Dasgupta, and Martinot emphasize that such ethical deliberation would have to occur during the preparation phase because it would be too late to implement it after a pandemic began. They conclude, "History will judge our generation's response to the next pandemic in large part by our ability to act ethically."

19. The list does not contrast or unify the major moral systems of virtue ethics, deontology, and consequentialism. I begin to do that in "Philosophy and Disaster," *Homeland Security Affairs* 2, no. 1, art. 5 (April 2006), www.hsaj.org/hsa/vol1II/issi/art5, and in chapters 2 and 3 herein.

20. The principles of no harm and well-being are related differently to this list. PNH is expressed by 3 and 4. PWB pertains to those aspects of planning in normal life that allow for self-interested choice.

21. John Rawls, *A Theory of Justice Cambridge* (Cambridge, MA: Belknap Press, 1971), ch. 1.

22. Winslow, "Triage and Justice," 143–54.

23. Baker and Strosberg, "Triage and Equality," 105–6, 111–14.

24. For emergency triage rules, see *Community Emergency Response Team Participation Manual*, developed for the Department of Homeland Security, U.S. Fire Administration, Emergency Management Institute, by Human Technology, Inc., McLean, Virginia, June 2003, Unit 4, Part 2. The published CERT triage rules for disaster are essentially the same as those used in normal emergencies. In the United States, individual states have emergency medical service protocols that are usually available online.

25. For example, prognosis for recovery may be part of a triage protocol. See, for example, Hick and O'Laughlin, "Concept of Operations," 223–29.

26. Such indemnification is usually secured with professional employment of rescue personnel and extended to trained volunteers in emergencies.

27. For further reports on the investigation of Boston's Big Dig construction project, see Matthew J. Wald, "Late Design Change Is Cited in Collapse of Tunnel Ceiling," *New York Times*, November 2, 2006, A17; Abby Goodnough, "Settlement for Company Charged in Big-Dig Death," *New York Times*, Dec. 19, 2008, A30.

28. Such triage would probably follow a calculation that future collapses in any one trip through the tunnel entailed an "acceptable risk." For a definition of "acceptable risk," see health.enotes.com/public-health-encyclopedia/acceptable-risk.

29. *Disaster mitigation* encompasses mainly structural aspects of preparation that will lessen the effects of a catastrophic event. See www.gdrc.org/uem/disasters/1-info-role.html.

2

Lifeboat Ethics and Disaster

Should We Blow Up the Fat Man?

LIFEBOAT ETHICS, MORAL SYSTEMS, AND DISASTER

Life boat ethics scenarios are the guinea pigs of moral philosophers. Extreme examples are posited, to which different moral systems are applied. The result of applying the systems is then assessed according to preexisting moral intuitions. And that assessment is presumed to reflect back on the goodness/badness or rightness/wrongness of the moral system(s) in question.

Philosophers traditionally support three distinct moral systems and use commonsense moral intuitions to criticize each one: *consequentialism, deontology*, and *virtue ethics*. Consequentialism entails that good results are the most important moral factor. Deontology, or duty ethics, requires that we always follow certain moral principles, regardless of the results. Virtue ethics is the moral system based on the virtues, or good character, of individuals.

In this chapter, I work through a number of life boat ethics/disaster scenarios: the fat man in the cave, cannibalistic speluncean explorers, traveler Jim, mercy killing after Hurricane Katrina, and the conscience of Huckleberry Finn. Each of these cases dramatizes a tension between the moral systems of consequentialism and deontology. The rules of Save the Greatest Number (SGN) and Save the Greatest Number, Who _____ (SGNW) appear to be favored when consequentialist outcomes of these scenarios are preferred. When Fairly Save All Who Can Be Saved (FSALL) is applied, preferred outcomes are more in accord with deontology.

Consequentialists believe that an action is right if it has the best consequences, or if it *maximizes*. It is assumed that continued human life and well-being should be maximized and that death and harm should be minimized. Consequentialism reflects practical commonsense intuitions. Every sensible and benevolent person wants "what's better" or "what would be best." This is why "The Greatest Good for the Greatest Number" is readily and plausibly adopted as a principle of triage and why SGN has a strong appeal in first thoughts about emergencies. Nonetheless, in both theory and real life, many are uneasy with a moral system that permits the harming or sacrifice of an innocent person "for the greater good." Most of us would not, for example, approve of a doctor's murdering one healthy patient to harvest organs to save the lives of six others who are terminally ill. We would prefer that the six ill patients receive their organs from either willing live donors or those who have already died. We assume that patience and hope will better serve the ill patients and the rest of society—not to mention the healthy presumptive victim—in the normal course of events. Still, a consequentialist could argue that ordinary moral intuitions against sacrificing a healthy patient are based on the belief that, in the long run, not committing the sacrifice will have better consequences.

In extreme situations, dangers may seem to compel drastic decisions in a short period of time. If consequentialist moral reasoning is preferred in those cases, it could mean one of two things: extreme situations justify actions that would not be permissible in normal times, or extreme situations merely bring out our underlying consequentialist moral principles in dramatic ways. However, in considering lifeboat ethics scenarios as cases of disaster, in the broader context of attempting to reason morally about disaster, the guinea pig role of lifeboat ethics scenarios drops out because disaster has a reality that hypothetical cases admittedly lack. Our moral conclusions about disaster are important and valid for contexts of disaster, in and of themselves, quite apart from what they teach us about moral theory. This is because disaster itself, in involving human life and well-being, is a full-blown and real moral matter—athough it should be noted that thinking morally about disaster is greatly assisted by the uses to which philosophers have already put lifeboat ethics scenarios.

Indeed, if we view lifeboat ethics scenarios as straightforward examples of disaster, they provide an opportunity to reflect on the applicability of competing moral systems to disaster cases. The moral system that seems most appropriate in such real-life cases may depend on our standing moral principles and the intuitions they generate. We will see in this chapter that ordinary intuitions seem to favor deontology over consequentialism, in the same way that it was evident in chapter 1 that egalitarian utilitarianism was favored over efficiency utilitarianism in cases of medical triage. But we will also see that there may be a genuine moral ambiguity about some extreme cases. It may not always be possible to extend a deontological application of FSALL to unexpected situations that elude the best preparation and preclude fairness. In those cases, the right decisions will depend on the degree of confidence we can place in the characters of participants and leaders, in their virtues. Virtue ethics is the subject of chapter 3.

THE FAT MAN IN THE CAVE

In "A Defense of Utilitarianism," Kai Nielsen confronts those he calls "moral conservatives" and "absolutists" by arguing that an example they would condemn as morally bad is in fact morally good.[1] Nielsen tells the following story (which he claims is well-known to philosophers) "of a fat man stuck in the mouth of the cave on the coast."

> He was leading a group of people out of the cave when he got stuck in the mouth of the cave and in a very short time high tide will be upon them, and unless he is promptly unstuck, they all will be drowned except the fat man, whose head is out of the cave. But, fortunately or unfortunately, someone has with him a stick of dynamite. The short of the matter is, either they use the dynamite and blast the poor innocent fat man out of the mouth of the cave or everyone else drowns. Either one life or many lives. Our conservative presumably would take the attitude that it is all in God's hands and say that we ought never to blast the fat man out, for it is always wrong to kill the innocent. Must or should a moral man come to that conclusion? I shall argue that he should not.[2]

Nielsen advises his readers to "forget the levity of the example."[3] (He should probably be excused for this because his article appeared in 1972, before obesity was considered a disease, making it insensitive to laugh at its sufferers.[4]) Nielsen reasons that while blowing up the fat man would be morally bad in itself, it is morally preferable to the greater evil of everyone drowning. He allows that killing the fat man would probably haunt all of the survivors for the rest of their lives and stipulates that the fat man be dispatched as humanely as possible.[5]

ASSESSMENT AND ANGUISH

One big difference between Nielsen's perspective and that of absolutists, who believe that it is always wrong to kill an innocent, is the time period taken into account. Nielsen's context includes what will happen in the future, after the fat man is or is not killed, whereas the absolutists are (presumably) concerned only with the time span of deliberation and immediate action, that is, with deciding whether or not to kill the fat man. A major problem with Nielsen's consequentialist approach is its assumption that the future can be known with enough certainty to override moral qualms about an action taken now. It is possible that the tide will not rise as high as it usually does, that there will be air pockets near the top of the cave if the water does rise, or that something else will happen to vindicate those who keep the absolutist faith.

Nielsen and other consequentialists could respond to this objection to their presumed knowledge of the future by pointing to the fact that most human decisions are based on more or less reliable predictions of what will probably happen. To evade an unpleasant decision in hopes of improbable events is to evade moral responsibility. The absolutists could respond that they need not hope for improbable events because the main moral aspect of the cave situation is that there is a choice. One must choose whether to abide by or reject the rule *Always Choose the Lesser of Two Evils*. And in making that decision, there is the further question of whether something's being the lesser of two evils does make it morally permissible, as Nielsen assumes.

Is it morally right to blow up the fat man in the cave? Is it right to eat the dead bodies of one's companions after a catastrophe if that is the only way to avoid starvation? Is it right to throw some people out of a lifeboat if the combined weight of all passengers is causing it to sink? Should we kill our helpless dependents if we cannot save them during a catastrophe, rather than abandon them to slow, painful death? All of these questions pertain to specific disaster scenarios. They all share a tension between doing what seems practical and following the rules for right conduct that we follow in normal times. These cases do more than raise the fairly simple question, How do we apply our normal morality to disaster? The answer to that question is easy: we should not do anything in disaster that would be morally wrong in normal times. Rather, the question raised by the disaster cases is exactly this: should we apply the morality of normal times to disaster? This question arises because if we do apply normal morality to contexts of disaster, the results might be great suffering or loss of life that is agonizing to contemplate.

The morality of disaster is a cause for anguish because choices are presented that involve loss, no matter what is done. Moreover, no two cases are likely to be exactly the same, so the kinds of choices required will need to be made anew each time. This means that moral agents are thrown into something like the reasoning used in case law as opposed to statute law. With a reliance on prior moral commitments and present moral intuitions, disaster situations may require assessment on an individual, case-by-case basis. Previously accepted moral values and principles will be highly relevant to such assessment, but we cannot expect them to save us from the work of deliberation and choice. Immediate intuitions, as well as strong emotional reactions, will be relevant, but we cannot permit the unfairness of arbitrary decisions. The following cases of the speluncean explorers and the longboat of the *William Brown* illustrate these tensions.

THE SPELUNCEAN EXPLORERS

Lon L. Fuller published "The Case of the Speluncean Explorers" in the *Harvard Law Review* in 1949.[6] As Fuller presents it, the case has been tried in the year 4300, in the Court of General Instances of the County of Stowfield. Four defendants have been indicted for the crime of murder, convicted, and sentenced to be hanged. A petition of error has been brought before the Supreme Court of Newgarth. In that petition, which forms the text of Fuller's article, the facts of the case are first described by Chief Justice Trupenny, and then responses are provided by four legal experts: J. Foster, J. Tating, J. Keen, and J. Handy.

The condemned defendants are members of the Speluncean Society, an amateur organization for the exploration of caves. In May 4299, five spelunceans became trapped in a limestone cavern after a landslide of heavy boulders blocked the entrance. A rescue party was soon dispatched. The rescue effort became a temporary camp of workmen, engineers, geologists, and other technicians. Fresh landslides occurred, and ten workmen were killed. On the thirty-second day, the men were rescued. But there were only four.

On the twentieth day of their entrapment, the spelunceans had established wireless contact with doctors outside to discuss their predicament of starvation. The doctors told the spelunceans that they would not survive another ten days without food. The spelunceans then asked if eating the flesh of one of their members would prolong their lives. The doctors said it would, and the spelunceans then asked if it would be advisable to cast lots to determine who should be killed and eaten. No one among the authorities was willing to provide an answer.

The trapped spelunceans then became incommunicado for eight days. When they were rescued, the authorities learned that Speluncean Society member Roger Whetmore had first proposed that they eat one of their number, then withdrawn his support of this plan in favor of waiting another week before committing to an expedient so "frightful and odious." Whetmore's companions nonetheless decided to proceed with the plan and included him when they drew lots. It transpired that Whetmore was the unlucky victim. So, Whetmore's companions killed him and ate his flesh before they were rescued from the cave.

The jurors' verdict was rendered in a hypothetical format. They said that they had found the facts (as described above, by C. J. Truepenny in Fuller's text), but they further found that if on those facts the defendants were guilty, then they, the jurors, found them guilty. The trial judge ruled that the defendants were guilty of murdering Whetmore and sentenced them to be hanged. Then, both the members of the jury and the judge wrote to the Chief Executive, requesting that the sentence be commuted to six months imprisonment.

At the time of the petition of error, which is described in the present tense in Fuller's story, the Chief Executive has not yet ruled on the requests for commutation. Fuller's legal experts raise relevant moral and legal issues, as follows. Foster begins by suggesting that the circumstances of the trapped spelunceans were tantamount to a "state of nature" rather than life in society under settled laws; he claims that the laws against murder do not apply to self-defense and suggests that the case of the speluncean explorers ought to constitute a similar exception if we distinguish between the letter of the law and its intent. Tating argues that Foster has failed to establish a coherent and defensible legal principle. Keen claims that it is dangerous to attempt interpretations of the intent of law and fill gaps one thinks one sees, as Foster advocates; Keen believes it is better overall to apply the law and have legislators change it after careful deliberation if some applications have unwanted or unintended consequences. Handy argues that the law needs to be applied with common sense, in accord with public opinion. Handy and Foster therefore believe that the defendants ought to be held innocent of murder, while Tating and Keen conclude that the verdict should stand.

THE LONGBOAT OF THE *WILLIAM BROWN*

This case is recorded in legal history. On March 13, 1841, the American ship *William Brown* left Liverpool for Philadelphia. In addition to a heavy cargo, there were seventeen crew members and sixty-five passengers. On April 19, the ship struck an iceberg 240 miles from Newfoundland and began to sink. The captain, with the second mate, seven crew members, and one passenger, got into the jolly boat. The first mate, eight crew members, and thirty-two passengers, got into the longboat, which was twice as many people as the longboat could safely hold. The remaining thirty-one passengers stayed on the ship and drowned. The captain told the crew of the longboat to obey the orders of the first mate as though they were his.

The longboat had a leak and after heavy rain began to sink. The first mate decided that the men should be thrown overboard to save the boat, and he ordered the crew to do this. Fourteen male passengers were thrown into the sea. The next day those remaining on the longboat were rescued.

The first mate and most of the seamen fled before the trial. Seaman Holmes was tried for manslaughter. The judge instructed the jury that the "law of the sea" required that passengers be saved before crewmen and that lots had to be drawn if passengers were to be thrown overboard. Surviving passengers testified to Holmes's compassion and bravery. Holmes was convicted of manslaughter with a recommendation for mercy. He was sentenced to six months hard labor, in addition to the nine months he had already served.[7]

ASSESSMENT AND MORE QUESTIONS

In the case of the speluncean explorers, the consequentialist principle of SGN was applied. However, because only men were thrown overboard in the longboat of the *William Brown*, an instance of SGNW, namely, "SGN *who are not male passengers*," was applied. Save All Who can be Saved (SALL) was not applied in either case because of inadequate preparation: the spelunceans did not bring enough food supplies; there were not sufficient rescue craft aboard the *William Brown*.

Each case was complicated in morally telling ways: the spelunceans included an unwilling member in their drawing of lots; no lots were drawn before longboat passengers were thrown overboard. Nonetheless, accounts of both cases reflect sympathy for the survivors, in part because they judged it necessary to sacrifice members and then underwent the ordeal of killing them (and for the spelunceans, eating Whetmore). Presumably, if Whetmore had agreed to be a candidate for sacrifice and the members of the longboat had drawn lots, sympathy for the survivors would be stronger in each case, and the legal rulings might have been correspondingly more lenient.

Without the unwilling aspect of Whetmore's participation, the question would have been only whether it is permissible to murder someone so that others may live, if that person had agreed beforehand that he might be the one killed. This would have raised the fairer, although still very difficult, issue of whether a person's agreeing to be sacrificed mitigates or absolves the wrongfulness of the sacrifice for those who carry it out. Along the same lines, if the seamen and passengers had drawn lots, then deciding who would be thrown overboard could have been done more fairly.

Fuller's scenario, as it stands, presents us with the difficult issue of whether we have a right to murder an innocent person against his or her will at the time of the killing, as well as against that person's prior wishes, to save a greater number of people. This is an extreme example of SGN. Fuller's case with Whetmore's participation and an agreed-upon drawing of lots, as well as agreed-upon lots on the longboat of the *William Brown*, would be instances of Fairly Save All Who Can Be Saved (FSALL). Both cases would still leave unanswered the brutal question of whether it is right to kill some so that others may survive.

If the spelunceans had had adequate food supplies and there had been enough rescue craft aboard the *William Brown*, orderly evacuations in both cases would have been instances of FSALLBP, or Fairly Save All Who Can Be Saved, Given the Best Preparation. But even if FSALLBP were always the working model for disaster preparation, actual cases might nonetheless arise in which unforeseen circumstances render the best preparation inadequate, leaving it to be further decided what fairness requires. The moral aspects of disaster preparation therefore ought to provide principles for situations of unpredicted scarce resources. That is, if all cannot live, who does get to live must still be decided fairly, or as fairly as possible. We can project a continuum of scarce resource allocation from some being inconvenienced, to some being allowed to die, to some being voluntarily killed, to some being murdered. The extreme of some being murdered is the worst possible contingency, and it merits our greatest concern.

In accord with consequentialism, a practical part of common sense would hold it morally permissible to commit murder in dire cases so that more might live or otherwise benefit greatly. However, what is morally permissible may be far from morally praiseworthy, and not all will agree that murder is permissible in such situations. The clash between actions in dire cases and subsequent legal judgment in normal times highlights the ways in which normal life supports a view that some specific kinds of action, such as murder, are always wrong. The question is not so much what people are likely to do when the survival of a greater number requires the "sacrifice" of a smaller number. History suggests that they are likely to commit the "sacrifice." The question is rather how their behavior should be evaluated when normality is restored and assessments are made within the normal legal and moral system. Fuller concludes his fictional account on this note of ambiguity:

> The case was constructed for the sole purpose of bringing into a common focus certain divergent philosophies of law and government. These philosophies presented men with live questions of choice in the days of Plato and Aristotle. Perhaps they will continue to do so when our era has had its say about them. If there is any element of prediction in the case, it does not go beyond a suggestion that the questions involved are among the permanent problems of the human race.[8]

Unfortunately, Fuller does not here tell us what divergent philosophies of law and government he has in mind or how they line up with the choices of the speluncean explorers. However, two related questions do arise directly from Fuller's story: First, should we give up morality when disaster occurs as a matter of general principle? The fact that in disaster scenarios some actions strike us as worse than others suggests that the answer to this question is no. Morality pertains to situations of human well-being, and disaster is very much such a situation.

The second question evoked by Fuller's story is, If we know that we will probably not do what is morally right in a situation because doing what is right endangers our survival, should we create exceptions to our moral rules before that situation occurs? If there is a prior consensus that our moral rules are not absolute but subject to exceptions in unusual situations, then we need to clarify what the exceptions are before they occur and make them part of how the moral rules are *specified* to fit particular cases.[9] The resulting specification that is applicable to the speluncean situation might be, It is wrong to kill innocent people so that others may live, except when limited circumstances and immediate human needs require that this be done.

Fuller's case and the situation on the longboat of the *William Brown* raise issues that require reflection and ongoing discussion. Even without consensus, clear, opposing positions would be preferable to the moral situation in which the participants in both cases, as well as their judges and jurors, are left. That situation is a consensus of shame attendant on the clash between practical common sense—kill Whetmore and eat his flesh so that more will survive; throw the men overboard so that more will survive—and the ruling moral-legal principle "Do not deliberately kill an innocent person." We could say that if some disasters require murder so that more may live, and if murder is believed to be morally right by those with the best intentions and information, in those cases there should be no shame, provided that SGN is the main moral principle. But if SGN is wrong in itself, or wrong when it entails human sacrifice, then shame is justified. That is, we could say that the moral principles we hold before disasters should be used in our assessment afterwards because morality requires consistency over time. There is nothing wrong with providing exceptions or specifications to our moral principles before the fact of a disaster and then applying those specifications when the time comes. But there is clearly something suspect in making up the exceptions and specifications in the moment of a disaster because that opens the door to mere rationalization and justification after the fact.

Nevertheless, we are stuck with the reality that although prior deliberation assists action and assessment after the fact, no amount of prior deliberation will succeed in reconciling those who hold incompatible moral principles. That is, not all moral deliberators will agree to the same moral rules, with their attendant permissible exceptions. Moreover, some dissenters may be less concerned about the factor of exception than other values. In this regard, Bernard Williams's example of "Traveler Jim" is instructive.

TRAVELER JIM

In normal times, received opinion tends to go against SGN and consequentialism when it entails murder: the murder of innocents is always wrong.[10] This raises the question of whether the consequentialist position is more morally convincing in extreme cases. In his critique of consequentialist moral principles, Bernard Williams has argued that consequentialist calculations may require an agent to sacrifice the connection between his or her identity and plans and projects, which constitutes that person's integrity. Williams's famous extreme case is Traveler Jim, who wanders into a Latin American village run by a military commandant. The commandant's men have captured ten Indians, whom they intend to kill. However, the commandant tells Jim that if he, the honored visitor, kills one Indian, the lives of the other nine will be spared. If Jim refuses, all ten will be shot. Williams argues that Jim has a moral right to refuse to become a man who has killed even one innocent person.[11] It is not difficult to identify with Jim, as a tourist, and agree that he should not be morally required to commit what would be a crime in his normal life. Notice that in this case, the issue is not whether it is right to kill one Indian so that nine will live but whether Jim has the right to be a certain kind of person.

Suppose that in order to survive himself, Jim would have to kill an innocent person. Does it make sense to weigh the value of Jim's integrity to himself if keeping his integrity would destroy its necessary condition, namely, Jim's remaining alive? The answer is yes, if there are situations in which we would rather die than continue living on the condition of committing morally abhorrent acts. Doubtless, there are such situations, even though people differ strongly, both as individuals and as members of distinctive cultures, about what they are. Disagreement over which situations merit sacrificing the lives of others so that more others may live may sometimes come down to this question of when someone's own death is preferable to continued life at the direct cost of others' lives. Notice again that the rights and wishes of potential sacrifice victims are irrelevant to this question.

The kind of objection to consequentialism raised by Williams shows that we do not all think that human life is always the highest value, so that the more lives preserved, the better. It follows that the types of situations that render human life—either our own or the lives of others—not worth preserving also merit analysis and discussion in moral preparation for disaster. Even if such discussion will not likely result in consensus or completely settle the matter, it would be valuable for what it adds to preparation as well as postdisaster reflection. Should those with whom we disagree act in ways we ourselves abhor morally, or should they fail to act in ways that we would minimally require, such discussion deepens understanding. Understanding can be a consolation, as well as a way to narrow the thought gap between normality and disaster. The greater that gap, the harder it is to recognize ourselves as moral agents when disaster occurs.

In the *Areopagitica*, John Milton wrote, "I cannot praise a fugitive and cloistered virtue."[12] Our virtues and moral principles have to be evoked and *applied*, that is, tested, before we can be confident of them, individually and collectively. But how narrow can the gap between normal life and disaster become so that the distinction between them still has meaning? This question is dramatized in the following Hurricane Katrina episode.

MURDER IN NEW ORLEANS?

On September 14, 2005, the attorneys of Lifecare Hospitals, which leased space to operate a long-term acute-care unit on the seventh floor of Memorial Medical Center in New Orleans, reported the following: In the aftermath of Hurricane Katrina, all of the Lifecare and Memorial medical staff were ordered to leave the hospital and abandon any patients who would not be evacuated. A doctor and two nurses administered lethal injections of morphine and Versed (brand name of the benzodiazepine midazolam) to four patients who, it was known, would not be evacuated. The patients were born in 1914, 1916, 1939, and 1944. The youngest patient, who was sixty-one and weighed 380 pounds, was conscious and alert. He had to be sedated before given a lethal injection. The bodies of the patients were found on September 11, 2005, and autopsies confirmed that the injections were the cause of death.

The doctor and nurses were arrested on charges of second-degree murder in September 2006.[13] The two nurses gave depositions against the doctor, but a grand jury refused to indict her in July 2007.[14] The presumption in news reports of the Lifecare injection case was that the doctor had killed the patients to prevent their suffering after they would be abandoned. In a similar case in September 2007, a couple who owned a nursing home in which thirty-five patients died after Katrina were acquitted by a jury in a trial for negligent homicide and cruelty.[15] The second case is similar to the first because deaths resulted in both instances. However, there is a considerable difference between deliberate, active euthanasia and "letting" people die, and the Lifecare injection case received greater attention.

The Lifecare injection case raises questions about our obligations to dependents if they have to be abandoned in a disaster. This includes not only the disabled and elderly but animals. Bonds with pets in present society are often so important that people will risk their lives rather than abandon or be separated from them. Although it was reported that fifty thousand pets were stranded during Katrina, it was also reported that many pet owners ordered to evacuate refused to do so because they did not want to abandon their pets. In October 2006, President George Bush signed a bill requiring that states provide for the evacuation of pets in natural disasters or risk losing federal money.[16] But the possibility remains that all animals will not be evacuated in some future catastrophe. Should those who will be left behind be killed? Animals are personal property, so this question might be left to individual owners to decide. But the moral problem concerning abandoned human dependents cannot be left up to their caregivers without prior moral deliberation.

Aside from the small possibility that one or more of the New Orleans Lifecare patients may have survived abandonment, the question is whether anguish over the impending painful death of another justifies what is called "mercy killing." The New Orleans Criminal District Court was not deterred from bringing murder charges in light of this question. Such legal action reinforces existing parameters of liability for euthanasia: what is illegal in normal times remains illegal in disaster. Still, the most agonizing aspect of

this case is that something not permitted can be very emotionally compelling. We are reminded that even in situations calling for great altruism,
our emotions cannot be our primary guides in moral action. The issue cannot be how we feel about the circumstances of others but what we and others accept as valid reasons for our own actions, apart from our feelings. Feelings are not irrelevant, of course, but they are not sufficient guides for action
because we have no way of telling from our feelings alone whether they are
genuine responses to the needs of others or merely reflections of our own
fears and desires.

Consequentialists support the principle that pain and suffering are intrinsically bad, and whatever decreases them is morally right. However, that
principle is not a universal moral rule; many would reject it if someone had
to be killed to end their pain and suffering. More generally, the intrinsic
badness of something does not mean that everyone, or anyone, has a right
to put an end to it. In the case of human pain, the liberty to put an end to
it is not legally supported in all places. In American jurisdictions that do
support that liberty, it is usually reserved for sufferers or their immediate
family members to exercise. And there are wide differences of opinion
about how much pain is worth suffering for the sake of continued life.

What kind of resolution between consequentialism and deontology is
possible here? When our actions affect others, it is important that we err
on the side of those moral beliefs that come closest to be being shared by
all. This means that we have a primary obligation to spare those who
would be killed or harmed by the application of moral rules that everyone
does not share. The broadest moral consensus for normal times holds that
we may not harm others, except in self-defense. Without comprehensive
discussion and argument to the contrary, people in positions of authority
over others are not permitted to revise this Principle of No Harm. Indeed,
it may be that the importance of the principle needs to be reiterated as part
of disaster preparation.

Nevertheless, despite imperatives to stay on the moral high ground, disasters have traditionally been viewed as episodes in which normal morality
and law are suspended, and that perspective will not easily be replaced in a
short period of time. Not only was the Katrina euthanasia case a subject of
public debate, but as with the longboat of the *William Brown* case, there was
considerable sympathy for those whose actions caused the death of others.
Some doctors, for example, said that even though the Grand Jury did not
hand down an indictment, the mere fact of a doctor's arrest for administer-
ing pain medication would make many health care personnel reluctant to
participate in disaster relief.[17]

Sympathy for the doctor who killed her patients and the ensuing medical
foreboding on the part of her colleagues is perplexing. Suppose that what is
morally important are good consequences and/or good intentions. The

sympathy and foreboding expressed set up a dilemma, as follows. The doctor who administered the fatal injections acted either rightly or wrongly. If she acted rightly, then her arrest (and subsequent acquittal!) should not deter others from similar action in similar circumstances. If she acted wrongly, then she should not be an object of sympathy. However, the situation is somewhat more complicated because some believe that although mercy killing is wrong in law and common morality, it is nonetheless morally justified in certain circumstances. That is, there is a conflict between received moral opinion and standing law, on one side, and private moral intuitions about desperate circumstances, on the other.

One way to resolve that conflict is to claim that sometimes individuals may be justifiably motivated (e.g., through overwhelming feelings of compassion) to act in ways that violate existing moral codes or that sometimes it may be right to behave immorally. This position is distinct from claiming that disaster merits a moral code different from the normal one because it would mean that morality need not apply at all to some disaster situations. The position runs the risk of destroying morality if many people act on it frequently. But it is a position worth considering insofar as morality may have limits. Jonathan Bennett's examples are precisely about such possible limits of morality.

HUCKLEBERRY FINN AND DEONTOLOGY

The kind of moral reasoning that philosophers call deontology (referred to as "absolutism" by Kai Nielsen in the fat man scenario) becomes sharply relevant when we think we might be at the limits of morality. Deontology, or duty ethics, holds that certain actions are never permitted (e.g., murder), and certain obligations must always be fulfilled (e.g., appropriate care of our dependents). According to a deontologist, if certain actions are morally right, then they ought to be done regardless of consequences, and if they are wrong, they simply must not be done. Deontology, in effect, yields lists of duties and prohibitions that, for the most part in normal life, do guide moral thought and action. Once more, the general question raised by disaster is whether extreme circumstances permit abandoning such lists. If the lists are absolute, then it is never permissible to abandon or even modify them—and yet people do so all the time. If the lists are not absolute, then they are even less perfect guides to action in disaster than they are in normal times. How do we know when—or if—it is permissible to put a rule aside or even modify it?

Jonathan Bennett addresses these questions in "The Conscience of Huckleberry Finn."[18] At the end of this essay, Bennett considers the World War I experience of the poet Wilfred Owen, who began his career as a soldier inspired by Horace's line *dulce et decorum est pro patria mori* ("it is sweet and fitting to die for one's country"). But sickened and saddened by his wartime experiences of suffering, Owen concluded that those words constituted an "Old Lie."[19] Bennett prizes what Owen called "the eternal reciprocity of tears"[20] and argues that we must be willing to test our morality against our sympathy. Even if our morality is good, which we will always assume to be the case because it is our morality, we cannot afford to blunt our sympathy because sympathy is what connects us to others.

According to Bennett, sympathy is particularly important in relation to bad morality, and he gives three strong examples. The first is Huckleberry Finn, who assumes that the practice of slavery and protecting the ownership of slaves is morally right. However, Huck's sympathy leads him to help his friend Jim, who is a slave, escape. Unfortunately, because he lacks critical insight, Huck concludes not that the morality of his community is bad but that he is, and he feels guilty. Bennett's second example is Heinrich Himmler, who rose to lead the Schutzstaffel under the Nazis and was responsible for the murder of four and a half million Jews and several million gentiles. Himmler believed that the greatness of the German race was the highest moral value, but he was also concerned about the suffering of those Germans who carried out the genocide and did not harden their hearts in the process. Thus, Himmler, unlike Huck, did not allow his sympathy to overcome his bad morality.

Bennett's third and most chilling example is the American theologian and essayist Jonathan Edwards. Edwards's bad morality consisted of a belief that humans were wicked and deserved eternal suffering according to the wishes of a pure and vengeful god. Edwards himself had no sympathy for the sufferers in hell and believed that those who were virtuous, such as the saints and good people like himself, were entitled to enjoy their own thoughts and images of this suffering.

Huck's impetus to help Jim escape, the sympathy of colleagues for the Katrina doctor arrested for murder, and Himmler's recognition of the moral suffering of concentration camp staff members are all examples of murky rejections of standing deontological systems. The rejections are murky because Jim should have rejected the moral system supporting slavery rather than conclude he was himself immoral; the Katrina doctor's colleagues should have been explicit about the principles behind their sympathy; Himmler should have questioned the moral system that gave rise to a bad conscience in those who obeyed it.

As Bennett points out, we always assume that our own morality is good. But sometimes extreme situations, as in the Huckleberry Finn example, themselves provide grounds for doubting our moral systems. However, there is a danger in using this insight to construct a robust claim that normal moral systems may be dispensable in disasters. Sympathy may signal the inapplicability, or even badness, of our otherwise chosen moral systems, but there is no proven and tested epistemology for how to weigh sympathy against what one otherwise believes to be morally right and/or legally binding. The promptings of sympathy vary so greatly—from motivating killing, as in the Katrina case, to aiding lawbreakers, as Huck Finn did—that prior rules for what to do when sympathy wells up are virtually impossible. Moreover, a lack of sympathy, or enjoyment in the suffering of others, as exhorted by Jonathan Edwards might just as well signal the limits of a moral or legal system.

We require that our moral principles be taken very seriously if they are not absolute. Exceptions are permitted—for example, killing in war or capital punishment—but they have to be broadly promulgated and widely accepted in democratic societies. If disaster yields acceptable exceptions to normal moral principles, it may be that in order not to destabilize the general principles they are excepting, they should be approached on a case-by-case basis as only *possible* exceptions. The assessment that they are real exceptions, especially if it is made after the fact, will likely have some basis in positive assessment of the character of those who commit them.

Virtues are traits of character that predispose those who have them to behave in certain ways. If we have the right virtues, if we can trust our own characters and those of our democratically selected and rationally chosen leaders, then we may have some confidence that we will make the right decision in cases that appear to accept our normal moral principles and commitments. The right virtues will dispose us to do the right things in disasters. The question now becomes, Which virtues are right for disaster?

NOTES

1. Kai Nielsen, "A Defense of Utilitarianism," in *The Moral Life: An Introductory Reader in Ethics and Literature*, ed. Louis B. Pojman, 237–51 (Oxford: Oxford University Press, 2004). Originally published in *Ethics* 82 (1972): 113–24.

2. Nielsen, "A Defense of Utilitarianism," 241.

3. See Nielsen, "A Defense of Utilitarianism," 248.

4. It may, however, be precipitous to relegate Nielsen's levity to the safely distant past. In January 2007, an obese woman was stuck in the mouth of a tourist cave in South Africa for ten hours before rescuers extricated her with pulleys and liquid paraffin. During that time, twenty-two other tourists, some of whom required medical attention, were trapped behind her. Internet reports of this incident freely made fun of the predicament. For the news story, see "Stuck Woman Traps SA Cave Group," BBC, January 2, 2007, http://news.bbc.co.uk/2/hi/africa/6225301.stm.

5. Nielsen, "A Defense of Utilitarianism," 347–51.

6. Lon L. Fuller, "The Case of the Speluncean Explorers," *Harvard Law Review* 62, no. 4 (February 1949), available at www.nullapoena.de/stud/explorers.html./stet/ (Thanks to Dave Frohnmayer for bringing this article to my attention.)

7. *United States v. Homes* (case no. 14,383), Circuit Court E.D. Pennsylvania, April 22, 1842, reprinted as "Seaman Homes and the Longboat of the William Brown, Reported by John William Wallace," in *The Moral Life: An Introductory Reader in Ethics and Literature*, ed. Louis P. Pojman (New York: Oxford University Press, 2004), 225–27.

8. Fuller, "The Case of the Speluncean Explorers," last page.

9. Specification is a method for making exceptions part of a moral rule, when there is a conflict between that moral rule and another of equal or greater importance. For a long-standing explication of specification, see Henry S. Richardson, "Specifying Norms as a Way to Resolve Concrete Ethical Problems," *Philosophy and Public Affairs* 19, no. 4 (autumn 1990): 279–310.

10. In a study of ethical choices by doctors and laypersons regarding organ transplants, the doctors reasoned with forms of SGN, or consequentialism, whereas the laypersons emphasized justice. See Robert M. Veatch, "Disaster Preparedness and Triage: Justice and the Common Good," *Mount Sinai Journal of Medicine* 72, no. 4 (2005): 236–41.

11. Bernard Williams, "Integrity," in "A Critique of Utilitarianism," in J. J. C. Smart and Bernard Williams, *Utilitarianism: For and Against* (Cambridge, UK: Cambridge University Press, 1973), 108–17.

12. "I cannot praise a fugitive and cloistered virtue, unexercised and unbreathed, that never sallies out and sees her adversary but slinks out of the race, where that immortal garland is to be run for, not without dust and heat." John Milton, *Areopagitica: A Speech for the Liberty of Unlicensed Printing for the Parliament of England*. From Samuel Austin Allibone, Prose Quotations from Socrates to Macaulay: With Indexes . . .—Google Books Result—Quotations, English–764 pages, p. 110

13. *State of Louisiana v. Anna M. Pou, Lori L. Budo, and Cheri A. Landry*, FindLaw, July 2006, news.findlaw.com/usatoday/docs/katrina/lapoui706wrnt.html (accessed June 2007).

14. Adam Nossiter, "Grand Jury Won't Indict Doctor in Hurricane Deaths," *New York Times*, July 25, 2007, www.nytimes.com/2007/07/25/us25doctor.html?_r=1&oref=slogan.

15. Mary Foster, "Couple Acquitted in Storm Deaths," *Register Guard*, September 8, 2007, A5.

16. Kimberly Geiger, "New Law Puts Funds at Risk If Animals Are Not in Disaster Plans," *San Francisco Chronicle*, October 10, 2006, A-2.

17. Nossiter, "Grand Jury Won't Indict Doctor."

18. Jonathan Bennett, "The Conscience of Huckleberry Finn," *Philosophy* 49 (1974): 123–34, available at www.earlymoderntexts.com/jfb/huc.

19. Bennett, "The Conscience of Huckleberry Finn," 11–12 (pdf format).

20. Bennett, "The Conscience o f Huckleberry Finn."

3

Virtues for Disaster

Mitch Rapp and Ernest Shackleton

ARISTOTLE ON VIRTUES

What is a virtue? The answer I would like to pursue here has not changed much since Aristotle addressed the subject in *The Nicomachean Ethics* about twenty-four hundred years ago. Virtues are dispositions to act in certain ways over time. Virtues are character traits. We are not born with them, but our nature does not preclude us from acquiring and developing them. Virtuous action is excellence. It both expresses and builds up our highest capabilities, thereby enabling us to achieve our highest end, which is happiness. Happiness is not a feeling but a quality of a person's entire life. There is no higher goal than happiness, even though we cannot aim for it directly. We can attain happiness only through the development and practice of our excellence, our virtues. A virtuous life is a happy one.

In early childhood, before we can reason, we are taught rules of conduct as a kind of training. Once we are old enough to reason, we are able to live by these rules and apply them to new situations. The practice of a virtue has two parts: deciding what to do in an immediate situation and then doing it. The virtuous decision requires what Aristotle called *phronesis*, or practical wisdom. A virtuous act is partly the result of a settled trait of character that is already the preexisting habit of the virtue. Consider courage, for example. An action is courageous if it is done by a courageous person, someone who already has the virtue of courage. However, a person acquires the virtue of courage by deliberately doing courageous acts. That is, one must already be courageous to do courageous acts, and the courageous acts are what make one courageous. This may look circular, but it isn't. The relation between a virtue and its virtuous acts develops over time, as the virtue is strengthened

49

by the accumulation of the virtuous acts, and the successive virtuous acts are prompted by the virtue as it grows stronger.

Becoming virtuous is a lived process. The accretion of experience never results in a mechanical or deterministic relation between a virtue and its acts because *phronesis*, or practical wisdom, is required to make the right decision about how to act, or what to do, in each concrete case. Aristotle does not clearly indicate whether *phronesis* itself improves through its exercise over time. But it is difficult to imagine *phronesis* as static because "getting it right" is a work in progress in morality as well as craft. Aristotle's example of the virtue of good temper makes this clear. The very complexity of being good tempered renders it an ideal, requiring continual practice. Thus, according to Aristotle,

> The man who is angry at the right things and with the right people, and, further, as he ought, when he ought, and as long as he ought, is praised. For the good-tempered man tends to be unperturbed and not to be led by passion, but to be angry in the manner, at the things, and for the length of time, that the rule dictates; but he is thought to err rather in the direction of deficiency; for the good-tempered man is not revengeful, but rather tends to make allowances.[1]

Aristotle provided a list of virtues concerning the proper behavior for tall, handsome, rich, well-born Athenian men. He thereby restricted virtues to what members of twenty-first-century democratic society would call "a privileged elite." But Aristotle's list can be revised or expanded, depending on cultural circumstances and necessities. Every adult can be viewed as capable of developing his or her own distinctive virtues in an appropriate context. Indeed, Aristotle's entire theory of virtues places human beings in social and political contexts. He thought that a virtuous society was required to support virtuous individuals and that political participation was an obligation of the virtuous individual.

Parallel to the discussion of lifeboat ethics in chapter 2, the main question here is, Are the heroes of disaster and the virtues they exemplify different from the heroes and virtues of normal times? In contrast to moral systems and principles, however, virtues are dynamic and creative. Virtues take on the unique individuality of those who have them, whereas consequentialism and deontology yield uniform principles of action that remain external to particular individuals. We admire and love our heroes as exceptional human beings, even to the extent of cherishing their eccentricities and frailties.

We are all heroes in our own lives, although it is difficult to view the drama and conflict of normal existence as exciting adventure. So, for the most part, we remain little heroes. Big heroic lives and actions have a larger-than-life quality, which makes it absurd to envy them and difficult to emulate them. Adulation by multitudes constitutes their glory.

Contemporary popular literature, particularly best-selling thrillers and science fiction that immediately express the geopolitical dangers of our day, can reveal more about our current preferred virtues than the people and actions we know and respect on a daily basis. Fantasy yields the big flashy heroes who survive and thrive under the worst events imaginable: bold warriors, steadfast soldiers of high integrity, and the classic explorers and adventurers of earlier ages. We want our big heroes' lives to have the honor and validation that we may feel is missing from our own. The virtues displayed by our big heroes are understood to be part of their identities. In early-twenty-first-century American society, popular entertainment and political edification burst with representations of aggressive, hypermasculine heroes, who display the virtues we admire for our times of crises. Everything they do is so up-to-date, according to the rules of its genre, that it is easy to be oblivious of the long history behind our preferences.

ACHILLES

Beginning with Homer in the Western tradition, the character traits of victors in war have been our preeminent cultural virtues. In the midst of a battle—of any kind—we are predisposed to look for a demigod who will sacrifice his life for a thousand years of glory attached to his name. Hector, the family man in *The Iliad*, is too tame to ignite our spirits. Hector's death beneath Achilles's wrath still horrifies us. We would rather not dwell on the gory details, although this can hardly be an aversion to gore, given how popular entertainment has desensitized us. Rather, Hector's defeat is humiliating to those audience members who are more like him than Achilles in their own lives. Hector is diminished by Achilles, frozen in the limits of his role as a good family man in comparison to Achilles's recklessly explosive star.

Consider this episode: Achilles has Hector on the ground. He searches for a gap in the armor Hector had stolen from Patroclus, the young friend/cousin/lover whose death Achilles is avenging. He finds what Homer calls "a most deadly place, the throat where the collar-bones divide the neck from the shoulders . . . the tender place of life, at the neck."[2] But Achilles does not cut Hector's windpipe clean through, and as he bleeds to death, Hector can still speak. He beseeches Achilles for assurance of a funeral by fire, to not leave his body for birds and dogs to devour. Achilles responds, "Would that I could be as sure of being able to cut your flesh into pieces and eat it raw, for the ill you have done me, as I am that nothing shall save you from the dogs."[3]

Despite the disgrace of Achilles's lack of compassion, it fails to spark enough indignation to smother our shame for Hector and his family.

Achilles remains the greatest of all heroes, his wrath still spellbinding after almost three thousand years.[4] Yet, in considering virtues for disaster, we should be skeptical of our own fascination with reckless bravery and ferocity. The issue is not only the spectacular destruction of human life but the personal authenticity of heroes who reject ordinary life in favor of a reputation sustained by multitudes of unknown others. We should consider the absence of inner experience in a hero like Achilles and how this renders him numb to the inner experiences of others. (Achilles suffers from his own losses, but his main response is destructive rage; there is little reflective sadness and no development of grief.)

The preferred virtues of a time seem simply to present themselves fully formed in the glow of public adulation. This is a phenomenon in democracies as well as totalitarian societies. A change in public sentiment usually requires fatigue from a war, shock at great suffering, or a major scandal. But those who have reflected on the nature of virtue beforehand may be less swept away by leaders who rise to great power on the crest of disaster. If the reflection occurs too late to fully repair the damage inflicted by the most recent Achillian hero, it may defend us from the deadly charisma of the next one.

The value placed on reckless bravery and ferocity may be culturally and even individually malleable, but what about those traits themselves? Are they not in some way inherent, as in "some are born brave, others timid?" Differences in human temperament are evident in early youth, infancy even. However, Aristotle's great lesson about the virtues is that in the process of deliberation, a person must know the self and correct against existing faults. Virtue requires self-management, particularly when pleasure is immediately at stake: "We must consider the things towards which we ourselves also are easily carried away; for some of us tend to one thing, some to another; and this will be recognizable from the pleasure and pain we feel. We must drag ourselves away to the contrary extreme."[5] Naturally having the temperament associated with the preferred virtues of a militant time may not be good fortune in the long run. Such a person may have to weigh the value of a long, full life against an early death with millennia of glory for past deeds and an unforgotten name. She might need to reconsider the value of ordinary life itself.

The discussion of disaster-relevant virtues for our times begins here with a critical account of Vince Flynn's protagonist Mitch Rapp, followed by Cormac McCarthy's man and boy in *The Road*, and concluding with Ernest Shackleton. I hope to make a case in favor of the virtues of integrity and diligence, as opposed to reckless bravery and ferocity, for dealing with disaster. While integrity and diligence cannot be directly attributed to Aristotle or his revival in contemporary virtue ethics, it should become evident that these are the virtues necessary for the conditions we fear most and that the same conditions that support bravery and ferocity can support their development.

THE VENGEANCE OF MITCH RAPP

Contemporary thrillers allow a vicarious enjoyment of Achillian rage without exacting its full price. The hero survives his adventures, so the audience is not upset and can look forward to the sequel. In Vince Flynn's *Act of Treason*, Mitch Rapp, an ultrapatriotic and fearless CIA operative, is called upon to investigate a car bombing that killed the wife of President-elect Josh Alexander during his campaign. The perpetrators are presumed to be Middle Eastern terrorists. Mitch is assisted by Marcus, a former MIT student (recruited by the CIA after he hacked into New York banks and transferred several million dollars to his own offshore accounts).

The car bomb that killed the president-elect's wife is traced to Gravilo Gazich, a Bosnian assassin now living in Cyprus. Mitch flies to Greece and watches Gazich kill two Russians, whom Gazich's employer had sent to kill him. Having thus taken the measure of Gazich's lethal skill, Mitch subdues him with bullets to his knee caps and hands. In the hold of the cargo plane transporting Gazich back to the United States, Gazich produces a plausible, but enigmatic, confession in exchange for the morphine injections Mitch administers to ease his pain from the gunshot wounds.

A set of explicit photographs are given to Irene Kennedy, the director of the CIA and Mitch's boss, by the campaign manager of the defeated Republican candidate. They depict the president-elect's wife having sex with one of the Secret Service agents on her security detail. Mitch discovers that Gazich's employers were Mark Ross, the ambitious vice president elect, Ross's unscrupulous campaign manager, a corrupt financier seeking a presidential pardon, and an otherwise principled homosexual Swiss banker. But Kennedy and Mitch decide that going public with the conspiracy would be too damaging to the office of the presidency. With the help of the Swiss banker, who will be allowed to live as a CIA "asset" in exchange for his cooperation, Mitch, now in Geneva, assassinates the financier and his bodyguards. Back in Washington, Kennedy poisons the vice president elect in the White House while serving him coffee in a room adjacent to the oval office. (Having accessed his medical records, she first slips him a drug to precipitate a heart attack, which masks the effects of the poison in the glass of water she hands him when he begins choking and gasping.) Mitch has to wait a year before Irene permits him to assassinate the campaign manager on his luxury boat in Puerto Golfito, Costa Rica. Mitch accomplishes this after consummating his relationship with Maria Rivera, a lovely Hispanic Secret Service officer, who was at first falsely blamed for the occurrence of the fatal car bomb.

As I hope the reader can tell by now, *Act of Treason* is fast paced and densely plotted. Aside from its value for long plane trips, it is an informative cultural document of the virtues in the forefront of American political life after 9/11. The value of patriotism is not merely absolute; Mitch Rapp's reckless bravery and ferocity render it thrilling. Mitch is not only unafraid of physical danger but unbothered by the bureaucratic mechanisms of due process. Assassination is more than permissible in this world. Even the CIA director is willing—eager—to assume its burdens, motivated by the same concern for the greater good that drives Mitch. However, their ferocity is also self-serving because, at every stage of their investigations and operations, they are more afraid of media exposure by opportunistic politicians than they are of terrorists. The War against Terrorism (a.k.a. "The Long War") is a real engagement for the protagonists, but they spend more time dramatizing its ideology than directly hunting and killing terrorists. The problem with Rapp and Kennedy as cultural heroes of escape fiction is this very evasion of confronting and thwarting terrorism as a menace to ordinary life. Terrorism is instead depicted mainly as a menace to privileged political life.

Throughout several more Mitch Rapp sagas, the most insidious enemies are well ensconced in Washington. So, it seems easy for Mitch and Irene to assume that once they know who the guilty parties are, due process is not only unnecessary but undesirable. Trials would reveal too much about how the CIA operates, thereby endangering its vital mission to protect the country. What's more, Mitch and Irene, together with those who work with them on a "need-to-know" basis, believe that ordinary citizens, who have not been "in the field," are incapable of understanding the urgency and high moral purpose of their work. This raises the question of how the sedentary reader can be counted on to root for them.

The sales of Flynn's books suggest that the public is very capable of acknowledging its general ignorance while valorizing those who violate its democratic values. Another way of putting this is that Mitch and Irene do not really think that all members of the public are ignorant of the importance of their work, only those who would oppose them through procedures of democratic disclosure. So, we are left with wily heroes who combine dishonesty with their other virtues. These shades of Odysseus are, of course, very good at preserving themselves while enjoying their own adventurous and, ultimately, evasive lives.

EPISTEMOLOGY

The main problem with the virtues of reckless bravery or boldness and ferocity in dangerous reality is their *epistemology*. Epistemology is ultimately normative because, more than a description of what makes true belief true, it provides rules for arriving at true belief. Democratic law has its own epistemology in the form of rules for what counts as evidence of crimes. Due process, or defendants' rights to know the charges against them, as well as their rights to fair and public trials if they dispute those charges, is also a form of epistemology played out over time through formal procedures. The structure of checks and balances, which ensures that the same people are not investigators, juries, judges, and executioners, is not only a way of taking care that only the guilty are punished and the innocent retain their liberties, but it assures that grave conclusions will not be subjective decisions. Checks and balances provide that independent agents and groups contribute separately to outcomes. The public nature of a democratic justice system, with the independence of its decision-making components, is analogous to the public nature of modern scientific investigation, with its duplicability of experiments by practitioners working independently from one another.

People who are recklessly brave find such rule-based systems inconvenient because the rules interfere with that straight, unobstructed line between what they think they know and what their impulses direct them to do, unmediated by deliberation. There is no need for Mitch and Irene to inform other skeptical officials of their findings because their supreme confidence in the truth of their beliefs effortlessly generates their recklessness. Such confidence is rendered laudable by a fictional universe in which events can be tightly explained by the motives and actions of a few selfish conspirators. Mitch and Irene's virtue of ferocity allow them to directly target evildoers who provide an unmistakable contrast to their own goodness.

Timing is important in a universe divided into those who are good and those who are evil. Ideally, revenge quickly follows crime to serve justice, prevent further evil deeds, and release the tension of heroic rage. It is even better if revenge precedes the crime. In Vince Flynn's *Consent to Kill* (2003), published just two years after 9/11, the spirit of urgency is set in a prelude to the main story. Mitch kills Khalil, a radical Moslem cleric, recently released in France and now residing in Montreal. Khalil has been observed recruiting young men, presumably as future terrorists.

Rapp stalks Khalil, knocks him down, and slams his head into the pavement. Khalil is probably now dead, but Rapp isn't "about to leave anything to chance":

Everything was done without hesitation and with great efficiency. Rapp grabbed the knife from his left pocket, pressed the button and heard the spring-loaded blade snap into position. Standing off to the right, Rapp placed his right hand on Khalil's forehead and stuck the blade into the man's neck just beneath his right ear. The hard steel went in with little trouble. Rapp then

gripped the knife firmly and drew the weapon across Khalil's neck, slicing him
from one ear to the other.[6]

Except for Khalil's inability to speak and the fact that Mitch's motivation is
patriotic rather than personal, the resemblance to Achilles coldly slaying
Hector is uncanny.

Mitch's world is replete with brutal episodes. A Saudi Arabian prince puts
a close friend in touch with Eric Abel, a former Stasi operative. The prince's
friend wants to have Mitch Rapp assassinated because he believes Mitch
killed his son in an aborted nuclear attack on the White House. Abel sub-
contracts the hit to a young aristocratic French couple who have become assassins in rebellion against their parents. (He enjoys the work, while she
would like to quit and raise a family.)

The French pair's plans inevitably go wrong when they bomb Mitch's
house. Mitch's beautiful wife, Anna, who is newly pregnant, is accidentally
killed, and Mitch survives. President Hayes himself authorizes what must
follow. Referring to Mitch, he tells Irene, "Unofficially, he has my consent
to kill anyone who had a direct hand in this."[7] Mitch's vengeance is again
terrible. Abel, for example, is left bound to a chair as his elegant Swiss chalet
burns around him. Nevertheless, at the end of the novel, Mitch spares the
lives of the French assassins, who now have a newborn themselves (named
Anna, after Mitch's wife).

The last twist of compassion is less a significant shift in Mitch's psychology than a hollow genuflection to family values. In Vince Flynn's universe,
there is no contradiction in the juxtaposition of cold killing with the nur-
turance of others entailed by family values. Irene Kennedy is herself the lov-
ing single mom of a ten-year-old son. There would be more consistency if
the summary violence against enemies were undertaken to immediately
protect dependents—which, to be fair, it sometimes is; most of the time,
however, the enemies are dispatched either before or after the fact of their
threat to the protagonists' loved ones. For greater consistency between family values and actions toward strangers in dangerous times, it may be more
useful to turn to thoughtful science fiction. But before doing that, at least
one objection to the foregoing due-process criticism of Vince Flynn's characters should be addressed.

In general in our society, the dramatic virtues of bravery, courage, and
quick thinking are usually associated with military or police action and
high politics in times of crisis. The boring virtues, such as integrity and diligence, which are necessary for careful epistemology and due process, are rel-
egated to administration in normal times, education, arts and letters, and
private life. The questions are, What, if not assassination, should be done to
dangerous, unjust enemies? and What kind of character, if not an Achillian
one, is best suited for carrying out the preferred strategy? It is unfairly easy

to condemn Irene Kennedy for executing the treasonous vice president elect instead of unleashing the turmoil of a widely publicized trial. Irene and Mitch know that Ross is both guilty of treason and likely to commit more of such acts, so why not simply remove him? As though to make this point, Flynn offers another challenge to the concerned reader in two excerpts from a forthcoming novel inserted after the end of *Act of Treason*.[8]

Adam Shashan, a Mosad agent, is working in deep cover as a janitor in Iran's major underground nuclear facility. Shashan reflects that Iran's only use for nuclear energy is military since it has abundant domestic resources in oil and natural gas. On the day before the night that Shashan has orders to blow up the facility, he discovers a threefold nemesis assembled there: the facility's director, Iran's minister of intelligence and security, and the murderous leader of Hezbollah in Lebanon. Shashan decides that he must take advantage of this rare opportunity and kill all three officials once they are in the reactor room. In this context, it is difficult to construct a moral argument for due process against Shashan's plan. Moreover, Shashan himself is, at the least, a diligent man, and his integrity lies in following orders in the service of a cause to which he is deeply committed. His impetuosity is merely a matter of rescheduling an event. But, the reader is also given a portrait of Azad Ashari, the Iranian minister of intelligence and security, as a reasonable and temperate man. Ashari himself reflects on the expense of the nuclear program weighed against an unemployment rate of 20 percent and the high likelihood that either Americans or Israelis will destroy the facility.

In pragmatic or consequentialist terms, destroying the facility might in the long run breed a greater threat than attempting a diplomatic solution, especially if Iran's nuclear weapons program is an ongoing internal economic burden. But suppose Ashari were an evil man and the nuclear facility were not an internal burden? Would Shashan's mission of assassination be morally justified? Are there some cases in which the absence of due process, although not morally good, is not bad either, that is, cases in which it is morally permissible? If the answer is yes, then the only way to approximate justice might be to insist that such cases be decided one by one by those who, in addition to being personally disinterested, are as far removed from gathering evidence and executing the decision as possible. To be fair, Vince Flynn probably tries to portray something like such a process in assigning "consent to kill" to the president of the United States. However, President Hayes is not himself a disinterested party because in *Consent to Kill*, he is already beholden to Mitch Rapp for having saved his life during an aborted nuclear attack on the White House.

Overall, Mitch Rapp's escapades furnish two considerations highly relevant to virtue ethics for disaster. First, Rapp's virtues, like Achilles's virtues, shine on a fast-paced battleground. For disaster preparation and response, there is little evidence that problems can be overcome by direct combat. The facts of disaster concern matters of survival. Unfortunately, on all levels of U.S. society, the immediate fear-based reaction to 9/11 took the form of flight from the realities of disaster into combat (i.e., war). If this kind of conflict continues, we should remember the important epistemological points: First, when boldness and ferocity seem appropriate, those who do the dirty deeds ought not to be the same people as those who decide that the deeds are necessary. Second, the decision that such deeds are necessary should be based on carefully evaluated evidence of the identity of villains and unemotional calculations of consequences. Furthermore, if the twenty-first century continues in the direction already portended, such that disaster and military disruption become our way of life, virtues that are less obviously glorious than boldness and ferocity might also need to be cultivated and valorized. In other words, when disaster becomes normal life, it might be better for its heroes to have normal virtues, rather than the heroes of normal life acquiring the virtues of disaster.

THE FAMILY VALUES OF *THE ROAD*

In Cormac McCarthy's 2006 novel *The Road*, a man and his young son undertake a journey south because the man does not think they can survive another winter in their present climate.[9] Throughout the novel, no one has a name. The man and the boy start out with a shopping cart full of provisions, trudging along a highway in a postapocalyptic world. The boy was born into this world, which is so bleak that his mother was unable to face their future and abandoned them to go off and die alone. The earth is scorched, most structures have been destroyed, those still standing have been looted and stripped, and the air is thick with lung-searing particulates. Nothing green grows, and the dead trees abruptly fall down.

There are other human survivors, but most are dangerous, and it is impossible to sort out the good from the bad before seeing what they do. Marauding bands scour the land, looking for food, their members "claggy" with the human flesh they have already eaten. The man has a pistol, and early in the story, he kills one of these cannibals, who has attempted to seize the boy.

The cannibal's brains explode over the boy. They keep moving. Once they are safely away, the man contends not only with the moral issue of having killed another man but with the ugly physical results:

> When they'd eaten he took the boy out on the gravel bar below the bridge and he pushed away the thin shore ice with a stick and they knelt there while he washed the boy's face and his hair. The water was so cold the boy was crying.

They moved down the gravel to find fresh water and he washed his hair again as well as he could and finally stopped because the boy was moaning with the cold of it. He dried him with the blanket, kneeling there in the glow of the light with the shadow of the bridge's understructure broken across the palisade of tree trunks beyond the creek. This is my child, he said. I wash a dead man's brains out of his hair. That is my job. Then he wrapped him in the blanket and carried him to the fire.[10]

The man and the boy continue their painful journey south, surviving on caches of food stored and buried sometime "before." The man has taught the boy that they are "the good guys" and that they "carry the light." The one explicit moral principle, which emerges countless times, is that it is wrong to eat people. The man is exemplary in his devotion to, and care of, the boy. The boy is both courageous and fearful, resilient and fragile. Part of his legacy is the absence of a childhood like the one his father had.

The Road is a very grim story, dreadful to read, but with its own imperatives for the reader to press on. The critics praised it for its depiction of the love between a father and son. McCarthy dramatizes and develops this love both as a motive for the man and boy to keep going for each other's sake and as a primary value that makes preserving their lives worth the physical hardships. Sustaining their lives requires the virtue of diligence because following the many rules for survival requires discipline. However, the principle virtue here is integrity. To preserve who they are, the man and boy's major moral rule is to avoid cannibalism.

The ancient Greek historian Herodotus, often credited as the first Westerner to voice *cultural relativism*, observed that in some societies, people eat the dead bodies of their parents, while in others such behavior is looked down upon. In a few contemporary indigenous cultures, ritualistic cannibalism is still practiced at funerals. But in Western society, cannibalism endures as one of our strongest taboos. In the 1993 movie *Alive*,[11] survivors of a plane crash in the Andes eat one of their dead companions, to avoid death by starvation in subzero temperatures. A member of the group cuts strips from the back of a dead passenger and lays them out for the others. One by one, they step up to partake, driven by their need but deeply ashamed at the same time. The audience is meant to sympathize with these reluctant cannibals. However, a contingent of passengers who originally wanted to abandon the plane finally does set out. They discover a lodge stocked with necessities a few miles away from the crash site. That discovery renders the acts of cannibalism unnecessary. Although this is a judgment of hindsight, it is just, given the survivors' general lack of enterprise and ingenuity. They are collectively passive and mainly wait to be rescued.

The man and the boy in *The Road* never waiver in their resolve not to eat human flesh. When they come upon a hastily abandoned camp fire, the man shields the boy from the sight of what is roasting on a spit. It is a headless newborn baby, presumably just delivered by a pregnant woman whom they had seen walking with great difficulty a short time earlier. We are given no clue as to whether the baby was stillborn or murdered at birth. In another episode, the man breaks into a cellar to find live captives imprisoned there as food; one denizen has raw leg stumps.

If we compare the moral status of cannibalism in *The Road* and *Alive* (and suspend our disbelief in the process of comparing "pure" and fact-based fiction), it is interesting to ask why the cannibalism taboo is stronger for the man and the boy, than it is for the plane crash survivors. One reason might be that the situation of the survivors in *Alive* is known to be temporary if they can be rescued, whereas the man and boy live in permanently bleak survival conditions. Eating the flesh of a dead passenger buys time until civilization can be regained, so it is an isolated expedient. But to eat dead humans either found or killed for that purpose in a situation with no hope of regaining civilization is to embark on a new, morally perilous path.

The man will not even practice cannibalism to keep the boy alive, and he always does manage to find a fresh store of acceptable food that will keep them going. He doesn't know that he will find it, but he uses his skills to look for it, hoping to find it. His integrity consists of this refusal to violate what he considers a core moral principle. Because the survivors in *Alive* will either die very soon or be rescued, their violation of the cannibalism taboo seems less important than it would be in an extended way of life. We can view them as minimally violating their own integrity based on the rule of *Just This Once* (JTO). However, if death were not a real likelihood, or if rescue would not occur for an extended period of time, then it would not be JTO. In fact, there is no way to know whether any given violation of a moral principle adhered to in normal times will occur JTO in the context of a disaster. JTO also presents the problem that as soon as it is accepted as a temporary rule for a particular case, there is nothing to prevent it from being generalized as follows: In all cases when the moral principle *Y* is applicable, do action *X*, which breaks *Y*, only if *X* is necessary and won't be repeated. Once generalized, JTO is more than a temporary or isolated exception to a more broadly accepted rule; it becomes a new rule on its own, allowing every moral principle one exception. Imagine if each member of a community took advantage of JTO and committed murder once! JTO shifts the focus from what is wrong to "what is necessary," from rules to their exceptions. While rules and prohibitions are clear-cut, one person's necessity for violating them may not be another's, and exceptions can therefore have an arbitrary nature.

The subject here is not which taboos ought to be respected no matter what—for instance, whether cannibalism is ever permissible. The subject is the virtues that are likely to best see us through disasters. The man and the boy are more likable and better role models than the survivors in *Alive* because they consistently remain loyal to their moral principles. They are diligent and have integrity. But they are fictional characters. For a real-life example of the virtues of integrity and diligence, we might consider Ernest Shackleton.

ERNEST SHACKLETON

In 1914, British explorer Ernest Shackleton set out for Antarctica on a specially built ship named *Endurance*. Alfred Lansing's 1959 account of Shackleton's expedition, also titled *Endurance*, is surprising both for what Shackleton did not accomplish and for what he did.[12] Shackleton had come to within 745 miles of the South Pole on a 1901 expedition with Robert F. Scott. In 1907, Shackleton led his own team but had to stop within 97 miles of the pole. The American Robert E. Peary reached the North Pole in 1909. Scott was outpaced by the Norwegian Rould Amundsen in 1912 and died with three companions (a fourth went off to die alone) before he could return to base camp. In the wake of these misfortunes for England, Shackleton's ambition was to achieve the first continental crossing of the Antarctic. He planned to sail to the Weddell Sea and land at Vahsel Bay with six men and seventy dogs. A second ship would land across the continent at McMurdo Sound in the Ross Sea. This party would leave caches of food and supplies on the other side of the pole. Shackleton's men would use these rations in the second part of their journey overland to McMurdo Sound.

In 1914, Shackleton was forty, flamboyant, and very eager for wealth and fame. He was highly purposive and relished extreme challenges. His men, in accounts of the journey reconstructed from their diaries and interviews by Lansing, all expressed admiration and respect for him as a great leader: "For scientific leadership, give me Scott; for swift and efficient travel, Amundsen; but when you are in a hopeless situation, when there seems no way out, get down on your knees and pray for Shackleton."[13]

Private parties, the British government, and the Royal Geographic Society financed Shackleton's expedition. Shackleton also sold the expedition's film and photograph rights and agreed to a lecture series afterwards. Five thousand volunteers applied (for token salaries), and Shackleton selected twenty-six scientists and seamen; a stowaway later became the steward. They set out in August 1914, and in January 1915, within one day's sail of their destination, the *Endurance* became stuck in the ice of the Weddell Sea.

Over the next ten months, the *Endurance* slowly drifted northwest until the ice began to crush the ship, which then had to be abandoned. Shackleton and his men transferred their essentials to an ice floe and began the process of killing their dogs, seals, sea birds, and whatever else could provide energy for their survival. When their floe split, they used their boats to find a second frozen sanctuary. They drifted on the ice for 850 miles until they were close enough to land for Shackleton to set off for aid with a skeleton crew. He and his two companions succeeded and returned for the rest of the men in August 1916. All who had embarked on the *Endurance* survived. (Even Louis Rickinson [a.k.a. Rickenson] the chief engineer who had a special aversion to cold, survived, to die at age 62 in 1945 as Engineer Commander on HMS *Pembroke*.[14])

What stands out in Lansing's account is Shackleton's care of the men and their care of one another. Despite the brutality of their environment and the continual uncertainty about their return home, pessimism and rage were not overtly expressed. For this, Shackleton praised his second in command, Ernest "Frank" Wild, writing,

> It is largely due to Wild, and to his energy, initiative and resource, that the whole party kept cheerful all along, and, indeed, came out alive and so well. Assisted by the two surgeons, Drs. Mellroy and Macklin, he had ever a watchful eye for the health of each one. His cheery optimism never failed, even when food was very short and the prospect of relief seemed remote. . . . The demons of depression could find no foothold when he was around, and, not content with merely "telling," he was " doing" as much as, and very often more than, the rest.[15]

That preservation of apparent optimism probably supported peace and order within the survival community. To the extent that such formality and forbearance was a continual, deliberate, series of choices, it represents the integrity of preserving normal standards of social behavior, comparable to the rejection of cannibalism in *The Road*.

It is also interesting how the men of the *Endurance*, like other chronicled heroes who have survived in harsh conditions, exhibited a strong desire to construct the basics of a home, a place to sleep and eat and store necessary items, from one day to the next. This impulse toward stability is another important element of the preservation or re-creation of normality under harsh circumstances. The home base or camp becomes a source of psychological calm, as well as physical safety, while it simultaneously supports the spirit of community. The endless hauling, packing, unpacking, checking, protecting, and repairing of tools and supplies, combined with constant attention to their needs for warmth and food, became the primary focus of Shackleton and his men. Making camp and setting up appropriate habits of rationing and physical care are also ways to change the environment toward one's own benefit, a "soft," or cultural, form of evolutionary adaptability. This not only exemplifies the virtue of diligence but expresses that virtue more concretely as *domesticity*.[16] Here is Shackleton relating the circumstances of his crew who spent four months on Elephant Island, while he was away seeking help for the expedition:

The first consideration, which was even more important than that of food, was to provide shelter. The semi-starvation during the rift on the ice floe, added to the exposure in the boats, and the inclemencies of the weather encountered after our landing on Elephant Island, had left its mark on a good many of them. Rickenson, who bore up gamely to the last, collapsed from heart failure. Blackborrow and Hudson could not move. All were frostbitten in varying degrees, and their clothes, which had been worn continuously for six months, were much the worse for wear.[17]

Of course, shelter in Antarctica is a necessity to prevent freezing to death and a way to protect those already ill from getting sicker. But beyond this, Shackleton and his men cared for one another with the same attention that ill and wounded people merited back home in England. If someone shivered uncontrollably, they massaged him to warmth; they dressed each other's wounds; food was scrupulously measured, rationed, and equally divided, down to the smallest scraps of meat, pinches of salt, and lumps of fat. This small scale of domestic detail, undertaken as much to support the dignity of life as well as to endure physically, is also evident in *The Road*, when the man finds new clothes for the boy, washes him, or gives him a treat. In both situations, everyone also does his best to take care of the self. To attend to such minutia in crude conditions requires a focused, subjective awareness of how existence *feels*. Unlike vanity or easy generosity in conditions of comparative luxury, the combination of self-awareness, concern, and humility in such ministrations attests to authenticity. It is authentic to react to how a human being feels, whether it is one's self or another. This is a far cry from the other-directed virtue of a strong and well-armed self-presentation that will support glory. It is difficult to imagine Achilles or Mitch Rapp cleaning up a human animal mess because their virtues soar above the simply biological—when they are not trying to destroy it.

Still, we need to be mindful that Shackleton and his men were also after glory at the outset and were very destructive in their everyday behavior on the ice. Shackleton and other enterprising adventurers like him had the privilege of support from those with great wealth and political power. Shackleton also had a constant, admiring audience, who, before an awareness of animal exploitation, overlooked the fact that the survivors of the *Endurance* basically killed every animal in range that they could shoot or club to death. Dogs, seals, penguins—if it moved, it was food. We also need to be reminded that Shackleton *chose* to test himself, as did his volunteer crew. He was of a stamp that lived out a tremendous sense of strength, God-given superiority, and dominion over the natural world, with unquestioned entitlement to everything in it. The entire project of modern exploration, for which Shackleton provided an exemplary finale, was predatory at heart.

Contemporary disaster victims, by contrast, are likely to be ordinary people with minimal survival skills. They quiver meekly before danger rather than rush to meet it as a challenge. Their lack of the classic explorer's sense of entitlement over nature is both a virtue and a weakness. It is a virtue because most do not kill animals as readily; it is a weakness because of their squeamishness and guest status in nature. Many are now physically unfit, obese, and dependent on medications for body and mind that no early-twentieth-century explorer could have imagined. Nevertheless, every disaster calls forth unexpected heroes, who rise to the occasion from this same passive mass. And the passive mass itself retains some hunger for testing itself against "the wild," even if only vicariously by viewing television shows such as *Man vs. Wild*, *Survivorman*, or the late Steve Irwin's *Crocodile Hunter*. There are, however, also cautionary tales for the sedentary public, such as *Lost in the Wild* and Werner Herzog's masterful documentation in *Grizzly Man* (2005) of Timothy Treadwell's spectacle of self-destruction.

For those who choose neither to test themselves without customary conveniences nor to acquire new skills for likely disasters, elected leaders and their appointees will need to assume responsibility. No matter how important the virtues of integrity and diligence are for individual cultivation, contemporary disasters require a broader public responsibility on the part of what is generically understood to be "government" and its public policies. Those obligations will be the subject of Part II.

But for those who do choose to test themselves or who find the government's best efforts insufficient to save them, the Achillian virtues will probably be less useful and less admirable than integrity and diligence. This suggests that the appropriate virtues for disaster are closer to desirable habits in normal conditions than they are to some radically different form of moral life. Integrity and diligence, unlike reckless bravery and ferocity, are not episodic virtues evident in isolated, glorious feats; they are daily traits of character, manifest in thousands of details of mundane activities. For prolonged conditions of deprivation and danger, integrity and diligence can provide a constant background support of life and its sustaining moral values. Against this background, reckless bravery and ferocity appear as occasional shooting stars, if not mere fireworks for a passive audience.

A NEW MORAL SYSTEM FOR DISASTER?

To summarize the discussions in chapters 1 and 2, democratic principles preclude overriding the moral principles of normal times in designing responses to disaster. Real and fictional case studies in disasters seem to favor egalitarian or deontological moral principles over those of efficiency or a simple utilitarianism that saves the greatest number. In morally ambiguous extreme cases, we do well to rely on the character or virtues of those in positions to make decisions, and this has been the subject of the present chapter. Because not all individuals are prepared to be so tested, political approaches are required, and this will be the subject of chapters 4 to 6 in Part II.

It is important to note at this point that nothing in the preceding discussion has supported the idea of new or different moral principles or systems for disaster. Rather, all of the published case studies and fictional scenarios bring existing moral reasoning from normal times to bear on extraordinary situations. This would seem to settle the question of whether we need a new moral system for disaster. While those who valorize the Achillian virtues of bravery and ferocity might disagree, it is difficult to imagine that they speak for numerical majorities in democratic societies at this time. Aside from increased reliance on the Achillian virtues or crude utilitarian policies of saving the greatest number in instant circumstances that could have been prevented with better preparation, it is not clear what a new moral system for disaster would entail. If the new system is constructed to justify actions taken in response to disaster that are otherwise not supported by, or even contradict, principles in existing moral systems, there is no reason to believe in the moral legitimacy of such a new system. If the new system is to be legitimately constructed before the pressures of this or that crisis, then the burden is on those who advocate it to present it, if not now, then at some future normal time.

NOTES

1. Aristotle, *Nichomachean Ethics*, in *Basic Works of Aristotle*, ed. Richard McKeon (New York: Random House, 1941), book IV, ch. 5, 1125b32–1126a103, 996.

2. Homer, *The Iliad*, Book XXII, trans. Samuel Butler. Internet Classics Archives, http://classics.mit.edu/Homer/iliad.22.xxii.html. For a slightly wordier translation, see the Lang, Leaf, and Myers translation (New York: Macmillan, 1930), 404.

3. Homer, *The Iliad*.

4. Brad Pitt recently resurrected Achilles for a mass audience in the 2004 movie *Troy*. Pitt's portrayal may be too vacuous because when merely pretty Paris, played by Orlando Bloom, brings him down with that arrow to the heel, there is no irony.

5. Aristotle, *Nichomachean Ethics*, 1109b, 1–4, 963.

6. Vince Flynn, *Consent to Kill* (New York: Pocket Star Books, Simon and Schuster, 2003), 33.

7. Flynn, *Consent to Kill*, 406.

8. Flynn, *Act of Treason*, see Flynn, *Consent to Kill*, chs. 2 and 4 in the unnumbered pages after 467.

9. Cormac McCarthy, *The Road* (New York: Vintage Books, Random House), 2006.

10. McCarthy, *The Road*, 73–74.

11. The movie was based on the book about the true experiences of the Uruguayan rugby team members who were on the plane. For information about the real events, the book, and an earlier movie, see www.gdaspotlight.com/PDF/1.pdf.

12. Alfred Lansing, *Endurance* (London: Weidenfeld & Nicolson), 2000.

13. Lansing, *Endurance*, 14.

14. http://www.coolantarctica.com/Antarctica%20fact%20file/History/biography/rickinson_louis.htm (accessed December 2008).

15. Ernest Shackleton, *South: The Endurance Expedition* (1919; repr., New York: New American Library, 1999), 260.

16. Sarah Moss writes in *The Frozen Ship* about a sense of "home" as motivating Scandinavian northern colonization, but that is a question of intentional, permanent relocation rather than the short-term survival virtue I am attempting to describe here. See Sarah Moss, "Part One: Making a Home," in *The Frozen Ship: The Histories and Tales of Polar Exploration* (New York: United Tribes Media, 2006), 29–57.

17. Shackleton, *South*, 445.

II

POLITICS

4

The Social Contract

Thomas Hobbes, John Locke, and Art Spiegelman

FREEDOM AND LIBERTY OR MORALITY AND LAW

Our autonomy, or freedom, is an internal, psychic matter, whereas our liberty concerns what we and others may and may not do according to the law. To continue the discussion of chapter 3, we are free to choose and develop our virtues, whereas our liberty lies in the presence or absence of external safeguards and constraints. However, the freedom to choose and develop our virtues is merely theoretical and abstract without consideration of the context in which it will occur. Aristotle could not envision the development of the virtues of the members of the privileged elite in Athenian society apart from a virtuous society. Not only was appropriate childhood training necessary, but the state had to be just to support the individual's virtues. Also, it was a virtue for the just man to participate in government and civic affairs.[1]

Aristotle did not simply relate the individual to the state as independent entities. He thought that man was by nature a political animal. After describing the origins of the state in households, villages, and other smaller forms of social organization, he considered it appropriate to conclude "that the state is a creation of nature, and that man is by nature a political animal."[2] Aristotle meant this literally as a characterization of normal human life and not only of human ideas and ideals. He believed that it is the nature of a "political animal" to live among others in a *polis* or city rather than alone or in small groups.

There are, of course, more recent metaphorical and theoretical connections between the individual and political society or between morality and the law that are directly relevant to our own times. We talk about living "under" or "within" the law, though we may not know what the relevant laws are that define our liberties. Most average citizens construct their lives with the intention of not violating laws—they generally intend to be law-abiding. Specific laws are often uppermost in the minds of those who intend to break or enforce them; criminals and police probably know the law better than the average citizen. Average citizens do not always need to know exactly what the law is because they are justifiably confident of being law-abiding. They assume, more or less correctly, that the law is more or less coextensive with their morality and that they already know the difference between right and wrong actions.

Morality is prior to law whenever particular forms of government are advocated or before governments exist. But once a government is established, law breakers are presumed to be immoral, and it requires a special effort to use moral principles to criticize existing laws and government, even in democracies. Still, the moral foundation of government and law is pertinent to thinking about disaster. Moral intuitions can guide the creation of new laws for unprecedented situations and/or be used to extend existing laws to cover them; moral intuitions may also motivate criticism of the laws applicable to disaster.

Since the Cold War, American presidents have issued or operated under Presidential Decision Directives that ensure the continuity of federal and local government under a National Security Emergency. Besides providing for Continuity of Government (COG), these directives have stipulated Enduring Constitutional Government (ECG) and Continuity of Operations (COOP).[3] The role of national-security directives in increasing presidential powers and possibly shifting traditional divisions of governmental power from the legislative to the executive occasions much ongoing debate.[4] However, there exists a consensus so broad that it is implicit: the U.S. government will endure during national-security emergencies and natural catastrophes.[5] Furthermore, this endurance will be continuous with a return to normal conditions.

Still, the need for presidential directives covering national security and catastrophic disruptions raises imperative questions: How will the government endure? What will be the effects on private citizens of diminished government functioning? Presidential directives seem to make provisions from the perspective of top government officials and appear to be primarily about the preservation of government. While current national-security directives stipulate COOP, it is difficult to distinguish within these stipulations between operations that preserve government authority and powers and those that directly benefit private individuals. From the perspective of citizens, the result is that although there will still be law—which it is presumed they will obey—their own active roles and the importance of their lives and well-being are not the main subject. Such omission of autonomous civilians, of their experiences, practices, and plans, in disaster preparation and response is not a possibility in real life. Government is already imbedded in the daily workings of society in normal times and might be even more pervasive during extended disasters. That is, these directives are too abstract in referring to government as a discrete entity separate from society.

How do we preserve democratic society in disaster? Perhaps the perspective of private citizens can be expressed in terms of a "trade-off" between security and liberty and an examination and reaffirmation of the values of each. Perhaps the real questions are these: How much protection from danger do we want for which we are willing to pay with the liberties we take for granted? What risks would or should we choose to take to safeguard our liberties?

These are vital questions, but they have less content and are vaguer than they appear. First, the "we" who will answer them and thereby be protected —or not—is undetermined—it could be our political leaders using discretionary or extraordinary powers, or it could be "we the people." In the former case, it is a matter of top-down executive decisions; in the latter, of representatives' votes, referenda, or, on a community level, even direct, individual, civilian choice. Second, the term *risks* refers to different things in preparing for, responding to, and preventing disasters. In preparation, at risk is the money and other resources allocated, which will have been wasted if a disaster does not occur; the liberty at stake is the benefit of property ownership of one kind or another. In disaster response, life, well-being, and property are at risk; the liberties constrained are likely to be more personal, such as freedom of movement and assembly, although prior property and consumption rights might also be curtailed. In prevention, the risk may be loss of life and property or the occurrence of disaster itself; the liberties involve persons, their property, their movement, and their privacy, as well as due process under existing law.

It is in the prevention of disaster that the trade-off between security and safety is most urgent, particularly in recent cases of the apprehension of terrorist suspects. If prevention is confused with preparation and response, then the civilian rights and risks in those phases are easily overlooked. In this chapter, I develop an optimistic application of classic social contract theory to disaster preparation and response. I then consider a dismissal from postmodern pessimists and attempt to address that position with the help of Art Spiegelman.

SOCIAL CONTRACT THEORY

For the United States, the idea of a social contract at the foundation of civil society, or society under government, dates back to John Locke and Thomas Hobbes in the seventeenth century. Of course, theirs are not the only ideas as to how government originated and can be justified. This chapter began with reference to the tradition of naturalistic political theories, dating from Aristotle's *Politics*, whereby government is understood to have developed from smaller forms of human organization.[6] There are also supernatural political theories, whereby government is a creation of God (St. Augustine[7]), and grand historical political theories, whereby government is the expression of other principles guiding the natural, human, and social order (G. W. F. Hegel and Karl Marx[8]). There are utopian, Manichean, and anarchistic theories of government, and so forth.

Moreover, Hobbes and Locke are not the sole architects of social contract theory. Thomas Aquinas, despite his debt to Aristotle, mentions the obligations of rulers in an early social contract manner.[9] Jean-Jacques Rousseau provided a variation on Locke's ideas in the eighteenth century, substituting the elusive notion of *the general will* for the will of the majority.[10] John Rawls, during the second half of the twentieth century, extended social contract theory to more egalitarian ideals than envisioned by Hobbes or Locke with his conception of justice as fairness.[11] However, Locke's version of the social contract is widely recognized to be the most relevant to the United States because his ideas influenced Thomas Jefferson and other founders. And Hobbes offers a contrast to Locke, based on a different view of human nature, which many still think best captures the difficulty and immorality of human life in all contexts, especially crises caused by conflict, such as riots, rebellions, and poorly managed disasters.

The social contract is an explicit or implicit agreement among citizens that justifies the formation of government and emphasizes the rights of citizens in their relationships to government. Social contract theory posits those rights of citizens that are prior to, and more fundamental than, the organization of society under government. Such rights are presumed in the U.S. Declaration of Independence and are protected by the first ten amendments to the U.S. Constitution.

THE STATE OF NATURE

The ultimate justification for the existence of government according to social contract theory is that government makes life better for those governed. Locke and Hobbes used the idea of a *state of nature*, a description of human life without government, to give an historical account of how government came to be and to explain its benefits. Locke thought that humans were cooperative and industrious in the state of nature, whereas Hobbes thought that their lives were "solitary, poor, nasty, brutish and short."[12]

Both Hobbes and Locke assumed that there was an original, ungoverned condition of humankind in the state of nature. But they also both implied that even if there never were a state of nature in human history, positing it afforded political theorists an idea of human life without government, to which human life *with* government could be compared and justified.[13] That comparison and justification is the main theme of *social contract theory*, which requires that government not be accepted as inevitable and beyond the control of those governed; rather, the origination of government, if not its continued existence, requires the consent of those governed.[14] This consent enables a social contract that places specific obligations on government (through which it fulfills its part of the contract).

Because life was tolerable in a state of nature according to Locke, he had a minimalist view of government functions limited to the protection of private property, the unbiased settlement of disputes, punishment of criminals domestically, and protection from foreign enemies.[15] Although Locke emphasized the importance of protecting private property, we need to remember that his notion of property was robust, extending to life and liberty as well as material possessions (or what he called *"estate"*).[16] By contrast, Hobbes believed that the competitive and aggressive nature of human beings required strong (what we would consider despotic) central authority to enforce the peace.[17] As a result, Locke defined the social contract as an agreement between citizens and their rulers,[18] whereas Hobbes thought that the social contract entailed an agreement among citizens to relinquish their individual rights to wage war against each other and at the same time agree among themselves to make an irrevocable gift of all those rights to an absolute ruler, or "Leviathan."[19] As a result, Locke visualized the consent of citizens to their government as ongoing throughout the life of government. But Hobbes thought that the original delegation of civic power to government occurred once, with no further requirement for citizens to consent.

Hobbes and Locke shared a strong conviction that the powers of government derived from the powers and consent of those governed. Locke, insofar as he thought that society could exist without government, believed that if government collapsed, its powers would revert to the people, but that if society collapsed, government would no longer exist.[20] Hobbes thought that peaceful and cooperative society, or even society itself, could not exist without government.[21] Both Locke and Hobbes were addressing the seventeenth-century Divine Right of Kings Doctrine.[22] Because, according to both Locke and Hobbes, rulers derived their right to rule not from God but from the people, social contract theory has been understood to be a secular political theory. Still, this is not to say that the most fundamental principles of government in the social contract tradition are necessarily secular. Locke's and Hobbes's ideas about government derived from Natural Law, which consisted of God's rules for men in the state of nature.

Both Locke and Hobbes began with Natural Law in constructing their theories about the role of government and its justification. The difference between them was that Locke thought humankind obeyed the first principle of Natural Law, that they not harm one another, whereas Hobbes thought that humans were incapable of not harming one another without government.[23] It should also be noted that social contract theory can be based on humanitarian premises that have no theistic foundation, such as moral intuitions about human equality and the intrinsic value of human life.

As observed, Locke endured as the political philosopher for the foundations of American democracy in those documents and legal traditions that both protect the rights of individuals and provide a method of decision making via majority rule. Locke held that citizens are entitled to representation in a legislative body and that the decision of the majority is binding on all citizens.[24] (For example, no matter how divided votes are along party lines, the winning candidates in American presidential elections become the presidents of those who voted for their opponents as well as those who voted for them.[25])

Nevertheless, Hobbes's view of the warlike and dangerous nature of human beings in conditions without government seems to have provided the most dreaded description of what can happen domestically, without adequate preparation, in the absence of functional government during catastrophe. As noted in the introduction, extensive data in the social science literature distinguishes situations of disaster from conflict based on cooperative responses to disaster versus aversive reactions to conflict situations. But the public continues to fear the possibility of postdisaster Hobbesian chaos. Such chaos is also a popular subject in postapocalyptic literature (e.g., in *The Road*, as discussed in chapter 3). Moreover, as we shall see in chapter 5, the U.S. Department of Homeland Security does not distinguish between disaster and conflict crises in its general organizational structure.

THE SECOND STATE OF NATURE IN DISASTER

Despite recurrent scenarios of science fiction, it is not only inconceivable but probably beyond the scope of political theory for any disaster to result in the total and permanent failure of government as we know it.[26] However, the temporary dysfunction of government in responding to some disasters and the different abilities of citizens to effectively respond to disasters on their own raise fundamental political questions that bring us back to Locke and Hobbes. At first, conditions under which individual survival requires private measures may seem like a return to a state of nature, however temporary. But this is not the literal case because present social and material structures have not only removed us from an original condition but made it very difficult to return to one in a short period of time. The inability to self-subsist in the absence of government characterizes urban subcultures in the United States, such as parts of New Orleans after Hurricane Katrina, as well as rural communities in parts of the world that have not yet fully industrialized. (Many residents of the Ninth Ward in New Orleans remained displaced and unable to return home for years after Katrina, as we will see in chapter 6; in the Jammu-Kashmir district after the 2005 Pakistan earthquake, millions were assessed as "completely displaced" by the European Parliament in 2007.[27]) There is every reason to believe that this would also be true of U.S. rural and suburban locations in the event of a prolonged disaster. That is, disasters that cause great physical destruction leave victims without the most basic survival ingredients in their immediate environments, in all places where they occur.

The destruction of an existing society's material basis of human life does not return human beings to an original state of nature because it does not return them to conditions under which self-sufficient survival is possible. It is not possible to return to some manner of living off the land after most modern disasters. However, the conditions of immediate environmental privation during the time period in which government is not functioning normally to repair material conditions qualify as a *second state of nature*.

The question in terms of social contract theory is this: What does government owe citizens in situations when government is temporarily dysfunctional in the second state of nature? If property is privately owned or owned by the local community, government does not owe restitution to citizens who have lost their property or had it destroyed. As part of government's benevolence, however, it is appropriate that it offer some compensation in those cases, much as a good neighbor might. The material resources of government in democratic capitalistic countries are the results of taxation, so such compensation amounts to some members of society helping other members who have sustained losses through no fault of their own. However, a more fundamental issue is raised by the inability of citizens to prepare systematically for, or take an active role in response to, disaster.

The material base of modern industrial society is a dynamic system that is kept in motion by exchanges through commerce. Orderly private commerce indirectly depends on systems of government regulation and oversight, while utilities such as power, transportation, and clean water and air, as well as protection and security, are more directly dependent on practical government functions and oversight. These indirect and direct dependencies on government have been broadly and deeply institutionalized in the very ways that render even a temporary return to an original state of nature impossible. If a disaster did not make it impossible to live off the land and the land itself were intact, a disaster could still make it impossible for citizens to function normally in society without government because functioning in society now requires the functions of government. Thus, while Locke could plausibly talk about society continuing in the absence of government, we cannot. In addition to the first destruction and disruption attending disasters, we face a second more profound breakdown in civil society, which is made worse by the dysfunction of government. For example, it is bad when people are injured and die from a disastrous event or are victimized by criminals afterwards, but these misfortunes are made worse when medical treatment is unavailable, human remains are not removed, and criminals are not apprehended and punished.

Disasters may block and delay transportation and disrupt the distribution of necessities. Civilians' resulting inability to create in a short period of time a useful social condition that will sustain their lives means that some will lie, steal, and kill to get what they need or to protect themselves. As a result, the second state of nature may more resemble a brutal Hobbesian condition than a peaceful, cooperative, and productive Lockean community. Such conditions of social disorganization require central authority for efficient reorganization and repair and for keeping the peace. Only government has that kind of administrative and physical capability in established leadership, access to relevant information, and deployable personnel. Because the second state of nature in disasters is only a temporary condition without government, not only does it not call into question the usual justifications for government, but many citizens accept, and some actively welcome, unusually strong expressions of governmental authority, such as martial law.

It has been demonstrated countless times that private individuals, institutions, and companies are unable to sustain effective long-term preparation for disaster response or to refrain from activities that increase risks in future disasters. Social scientists and public-policy experts refer to stages in disaster response that range from high readiness to complacent ignorance as the time after any particular disaster increases.[28] Structures washed away in floods may be replaced by more expensive ones that are just as vulnerable; brick buildings may not be retrofitted to prepare for predicted earthquakes; local emergency-response resources may be at the mercy of fluctuating local budgets; individuals may misplace, use up, or fail to procure emergency supplies; and so forth.

However, the general failure in civilian disaster preparation does not in itself imply that government must be the preparer or responder of last resort. Such a last-resort role is not, strictly speaking, a governmental obligation. Any obligation of government concerning second states of nature would have to stem from the basic principles of social contract theory. The argument based on social contract theory for governmental obligation to assist civilians in effective disaster preparation and response is this: Government has a continual obligation to benefit those governed by rendering them better off than they would have been in the first state of nature. The temporary dysfunction of government in disasters results in a second state of nature for those governed. Therefore, government has an extended obligation to render citizens better off than they may otherwise be in a second state of nature. That is, government is obligated to ensure adequate disaster preparation and planning for all probable disasters in precisely those ways in which the public has demonstrated its inabilities. The scholarly foundations for such an obligation would consist of new work in political science, political philosophy, and law. Here, it is worth noting that governmental obligations based on an original social contract, as extended to a second state of nature, are different in principle from special entitlements for some citizens, paternalism, or any form of socialist welfare.

HOBBES AND LOCKE POSTDISASTER

Locke's and Hobbes's contrasting views of human nature seem relevant to the kind of life possible in contemporary disaster. Locke believed that orderly and cooperative society, as he knew it, would continue to exist in the absence of government because he believed that we are cooperative and peaceful by nature; the state of nature for Locke was a viable social condition, complete with orderly market conditions and respect for private property.[29] Hobbes believed that orderly and cooperative society was completely dependent on government because he believed that we are competitive and aggressive by nature; according to Hobbes, we are not naturally social. Thus, for Locke, if the government is destroyed, normal society remains intact, whereas for Hobbes, if the government is destroyed, there is no normal society, and we are back to "solitary, poor, nasty, brutish and short" lives, a war of each against all and vice versa.

A present Lockean view of intact normal society under conditions of disaster points to voluntary, familial, and community organization that would regroup or spring up during the temporary dysfunction of government. Hobbes's view is the worst-case scenario, and it lurks as a possibility immediately following catastrophic incidents in the absence of adequate preparation and response. However, regardless of whether humankind "really" is by nature peaceful and cooperative or warlike, we already have enough examples of volunteer response and familial and community organization following disasters to view them as ideals during preparation. Still, there is no guarantee, even with adequate preparation, that such conditions will automatically prevail—all that can be done beforehand is to maximize the chances that they will. Locke's vision of a peaceful, cooperative, and, it should be emphasized, *self-sufficient agrarian* society, before government, allowed him to posit government as a convenience instituted mainly to punish criminals fairly.[30] In our second state of nature, government is a necessity for survival, not so much because of human aggression, although that is always a consideration, but because humankind can no longer get its living directly from nature in the absence of government.

THE SECOND STATE OF NATURE IN THEORY

The second state of nature as the result of disaster is both a possible condition that could become actual and a theoretical one. Preparation and reflection before the fact of disaster allow for the likelihood of a more agreeable second state of nature in the event of disaster. This is the second state of nature as a possible condition. However, the theoretical value of the second state of nature is severely compromised in comparison to the first state of nature. Political philosophers posited the state of nature as both an early historical condition of mankind and a general condition without government against which government should be justified. The requirement that government be justified derived from the voluntary actions of citizens living in a state of nature to accept or institute government. In the seventeenth century, modern government was in its early stages, so it made sense that Locke and Hobbes would describe the state of nature as a condition that plausibly existed in the past, just beyond recorded history. The condition in which humans were closer to a natural environment was also not completely overcome by seventeenth-century technology. We, in contrast, can no longer inhabit the earth as a natural environment but require human-made intermediary conditions between us and nature for our very survival. This means that in a second state of nature, without preparation, we are left to devise a precarious existence in dysfunctional artificial environments.

Not only do second states of nature fail to return us to original situations of material self-sufficiency, but they also do not place us in a political situation from which we can consent to government anew. Insofar as disaster results only in the temporary suspension or dysfunction of government, the idea of a second state of nature cannot be used to think about founding government itself as an institution that did not exist previously. The first obvious reason is that legitimate government still exists. But there is a second more important reason why the idea of a second state of nature cannot be used to justify government as an institution that does not already exist. Social contract theory requires a contract. A contract requires a lack of constraint on both sides. Because normal existence, and in some cases life itself, without functional government is not possible in a second state of nature, those governed would not be free to desist from a social contract originating government. They could not voluntarily accept or institute government, as they were imagined to have done in the first state of nature. Therefore, second states of nature cannot give rise to new consensual social contracts that found government.

Second states of nature can become bearable via an extension of preexisting government based on the original social contract conceptualized as having been founded in the first state of nature. This is why COG and COOP are so important. Without COG and COOP, whatever new government arises in the second state of nature will not be based on a consensual social contract as traditionally understood. It will not likely be either democratic or representational, and it will not have a moral foundation based on the prior freedom of those governed. Nevertheless, unless the support of adequate disaster preparation by civilians is a recognized obligation of government, understood to derive from the founding social contract, the public will be left out of COG and COOP, undermining the continuity and operations of specifically *democratic* government.

Without adequate preparation, government will need to play a humanitarian role in disaster response. Humanitarian aid is by definition unilateral rather than contractual. It is morally good but not morally required. Humanitarian aid from government to its own citizens cannot be justified in the fundamental way deriving from the founding social contract that obligatory government assistance in preparation can. This is because, theoretically, those governed, as contractual parties, actively participated in the original founding of government, whereas those receiving humanitarian aid are passive recipients. Humanitarian aid, although a kind, benevolent, or charitable response to need and requests, can never rise to that support of human autonomy that fulfillment of an obligation can. When obligations are fulfilled, rights are recognized. A recognized right to assistance in preparing for disaster not only mitigates the effects of disaster on human life and physical well-being but preserves human dignity.

In the Shadow of No Towers

It is optimistic to assume not only that the original social contract, based on the consent of those governed, is still recognized but that it could be binding for disaster policies. In presenting the foregoing ideas during recent conference travels in both the United States and Europe, I have encountered a combination of abstract agreement with the moral aspects of the originating social contract and its continued force as an ideal and dismissal of the present reality of a democratic social contract. The dismissal seems to originate from a general, pessimistic, postmodern perspective that can be summarized as follows:

> The activities of the Bush administration after 9/11, in apprehending terrorist suspects, using torture, and prosecuting the interests of global capitalism, have changed the meaning of "democracy." The word "democracy" now means "whatever panders to resource-devouring, planet-destroying, end consumers and their profit-greedy suppliers." Since how a word is used constitutes its meaning, democracy no longer means "liberty." Therefore, the idea of a social contract, whereby government is morally based on the consent of those governed and exists for their well-being, is a quaint article of anachronistic propaganda.

This pessimistic perspective is not coherent. If democracy no longer means what it traditionally has, then there is no basis on which to criticize undemocratic or fundamentally immoral government. If respect for human rights and the will and consent of those governed—which is what democracy has always meant—is abandoned along with "democracy," then what new ideal do these pessimistic critics strive for? Democracy has always entailed more than the word democracy. If some have misused the word democracy, that is no reason to turn against or dismiss what it stands for. This countercriticism now leads back to the moral foundations of democracy in a social contract.[31]

For an accessible and trenchant contemporary reaffirmation of the ongoing reality of democracy, we might consider Art Spiegelman's graphic novel *In the Shadow of No Towers* (2004),[32] which contains ten large-scale cardboard pages, each in color newsprint format, depicting 9/11's effects on him. These pages are followed by Spiegelman's politically nuanced history of newspaper comic strips, with reproductions of early-twentieth-century comic strips that are strangely prescient of 9/11 and its aftermath. The whole book is droll and self-reflexive, as well as self-reflective; it would be difficult to claim that it presents a naïve view of either recent politics or present reality.

Spiegelman has drawn cartoons and covers for the *New Yorker* magazine for over a decade, but he claims that political cartoon strips, especially in the old-fashioned narrative format he emulates in *In the Shadow of No Towers*, are very labor intensive. Although he originally planned a weekly series of the 9/11 material, some of the pages took him five weeks each, so they were first published in Germany's weekly broadsheet newspaper *Die Zeit* and later in New York's weekly *Forward*. Spiegelman welcomed these publication venues because he found that soon after 9/11, during a time of patriotic fervor, the *New Yorker*, *New York Review of Books*, and *New York Times*, all of which had previously solicited work from him, had no interest in his posttraumatic expressions. Americans were then living in almost constant fear—of more terrorist hijackings, dirty bombs, anthrax, and explosions of government buildings and civil infrastructure—and almost everyone seemed to support the government without qualification.[33] By the fall of 2003, in what Spiegelman calls "the pre-election sobering-up period," normal political criticism reemerged. Spiegelman and others could then be publicly quoted as fearing their own government as much as al-Qaeda. Spiegelman explains at the close of his introduction,

> Still, time keeps flying and even the New Normal grows old. My strips are now a slow-motion diary of what I experienced while seeking some provisional equanimity—though three years later I'm still ready to lose it all at the mere drop of a hat or a dirty bomb. I still believe the world is ending, but I concede that it seems to be ending more slowly than I once thought so I figured I'd make a book.[34]

Indeed. And Spiegelman's "book" was not exactly smuggled out of a gulag or a dungeon for political dissenters. Political criticism continues to be open and robust. It presents new opportunities for fame and wealth and has become a distinct subject of journalism and best-selling nonfiction. Some of this criticism comes from members of the political establishment, some from an intelligentsia still proud of remaining outside "the system." If the existence of free speech is evidence for the continued existence of democracy, then contra the postmodern pessimists, democracy remains more than a rhetorical tool.[35] The 2004 elections that resulted in a Democratic U.S. Congress demonstrated that we do still have free elections—more evidence that democracy lives. And, the recent contest between Hillary Clinton and Barak Obama for the Democratic presidential nomination further corroborates the survival of democracy—as does Obama's landslide presidential victory. But, and this is a big question, we do not know if the criticism now being voiced will be effective, or if a future American presidential administration will do better "in the shadow of no towers."

Spiegelman's title refers both to the literal absence of the Twin Towers of New York City's World Trade Center after 9/11 and to the historical effects of the sole global superpower sustaining substantial terrorist attacks on its own soil. The condition of living under the shadow of the attacks remains unalleviated by the fact that Osama Bin Laden was apparently just as surprised as Americans by the towers' collapse.[36] As perspective becomes more nuanced over time, it is important to add to the mix of that which remains to be processed this dimension of unpredictability for even the perpetrators of disaster. Much of the political reaction to 9/11 proceeded *as though al-Qaeda was known to have planned the collapse of the towers*. But, here is how *The 9/11 Commission Report*'s ten writers, half Democrats and half Republicans, described the attacks:

> The 9-11 attack was an event of surpassing disproportion. America had suffered surprise attacks before—Pearl Harbor is one well-known case, the 1950 Chinese attack in Korea another. But these were attacks by major powers.

While by no means as threatening as Japan's act of war, the 9-11 attack was in some ways more devastating. It was carried out by a tiny group of people, not enough to man a full platoon. Measured on a governmental scale the resources behind it were trivial. The group itself was dispatched by an organization based in one of the poorest, most remote, and least industrialized countries on earth. This organization recruited a mixture of young fanatics and highly educated zealots who could not find suitable places in their home societies or were driven from them.[37]

In terms of disaster and devastation, it makes no difference if the collapse of the towers had been planned beforehand or was an unforeseen effect. In a way, the catastrophe's unplanned nature is more frightening than a meticulously planned event might have been. It raises the specter of sudden, unforeseen, and possibly unforeseeable danger and destruction that prevents a complete return to the complacency that before felt so appropriate to so many. And this means that preparation is all the more important because, even though it may never be complete, there are substantial degrees of incompleteness. It is both impossible to prepare for every conceivable disaster and undesirable for our society to realign itself pessimistically around the importance of disaster preparation as a primary social good. But core elements of adequate responses to even very different kinds of disasters allow for general preparation. Prudence, analogous to its place as a virtue in private life, could become a part of good government without crushing general optimism about the future (when we do have that).

The 9/11 Commission Report

Returning again to the question of whether democratic political structures are still in existence in the United States so that it makes sense to talk about social contract theory, the general diagnosis of *The 9/11 Commission Report* is instructive. The committee noted that by the end of President Clinton's administration, terrorist attacks were considered a threat, and Bin Laden had been identified as a specific danger. However, the committee went on to claim that the Counterterrorism Center lacked imagination in developing scenarios of hijacked planes and strategies to address them. While the CIA had informative, small-scale intelligence on individual Middle Eastern terrorists, it did not have adequate communication with the FBI. Most experts assumed that attacks on the United States by hijacked planes would enter the United States from abroad. Moreover, the Federal Aviation Administration did not have a fully developed system for screening items brought onto planes. Overall, in the committee's view, not only was the American intelligence and security apparatus uncoordinated as a whole, but it was still operating on a model appropriate to the Cold War.[38]

Aware of its own hindsight, the committee concluded that it would be impossible to protect Americans from all terrorist attacks, anywhere, at all times. Nevertheless, its general recommendation reads very clearly as an affirmation of the accountability, as well as the protective obligations, of government to those governed:

> The American people are entitled to expect their government to do its very best. They should expect that officials will have realistic objectives, clear guidance, and effective organization. They are entitled to see some standards for performance so they can judge, with the help of their elected representatives, whether the objectives are being met.[39]

If the people are entitled, then the government is obligated. While the postmodern critic may continue to eschew this language of democracy, the concept (meaning) of democracy not only remains in use but is necessary to criticize and correct abuses that falsely appropriate its name.

However, the best administrative organization and objectives to prevent disaster, with a corresponding public policy of honest disclosure, are insufficient without adequate public policies for disaster preparation and response. It cannot be known that the best efforts will provide complete safety but if effective and just public policies are crafted, ensuing failures will not be cause for moral anguish. Several aspects of such just and effective public policies will be the focus of the concluding two chapters.

NOTES

1. Aristotle, "Nichomachean Ethics," in *Basic Works of Aristotle*, ed. Richard McKeon (New York: Random House, 1941), book X, ch. 9, 1179b–1181, 1108–12.

2. Aristotle, "Politics," in McKeon, *Basic Works*, book V, ch. 10, 1253a36–38, 1129.

3. George W. Bush issued National Security Presidential Directive/NSPD 51, which is also Homeland Security Presidential Directive/HSPD 20, on May 9, 2007. See www.whitehouse.gov/news/releases/2007/05/20070509-12.html. This 2007 directive revokes its predecessor, Presidential Decision Directive 67 of October 21, 1998 (www.fas.org/irp/offdocs/pdd/pdd-67.htm).

4. See, e.g., Vikki Gordon, "The Law: Unilaterally Shaping U.S. National Security Policy: The Role of National Security Directives," *Presidential Studies Quarterly* 37, no. 2 (June 2007): 349–67.

5. National catastrophes are explicitly included in the language of the May 9, 2007, presidential decision directive (see note 3). The inability of some courts to function, in Alabama, Louisiana, and Mississippi, during Hurricane Katrina focused attention on COOP planning at local levels, according to guidelines issued by the Administrative Office of the United States Courts. (See R. E. Petersen, "Emergency Preparedness and Continuity of Operations [COOP] in the Federal Judiciary," 109th Congress, CRS Report RL31857 (Updated August 3, 2003.)

6. Aristotle, "Politics," in *The Basic Works of Aristotle*, ed. Richard McKeon (New York: Random House, 1941), book I, 1252–53.

7. St. Augustine, *The City of God*, ed. R. W. Dyson (Cambridge, UK: Cambridge University Press, 1998).

8. Wolfgang Hegel, *Philosophy of Right and Law*, trans. J. M. Sterrett and Carl J. Friedrich, in *The Philosophy of Hegel*, ed. Carl J. Friedrich (New York: Random House, 1953). Karl Marx and Friedrich Engels, "The Communist Manifesto," in *Karl Marx, Selected Writings*, ed. Lawrence H. Simon (Indianapolis, IN: Hackett, 1994), 153–86.

9. Thomas Aquinas, *On Kingship*, trans. G. B. Phelan and I. Th. Eschmann (Toronto: Pontifical Institute of Medieval Studies, 1959), book I, ch. 5.

10. It's difficult to identify precisely what Rousseau means by the general will in the abstract because he says it is not the same as majority rule, and we do associate majority rule with democracy. However, in practical organizations, such as work units or families, it is sometimes evident that following the will of the majority, or even granting each participant what she wants, is destructive to the well-being of the whole group as an entity. This is because the whole group will outlast individual members and because majority or individual interests may not provide for a context of support and freedom that will benefit each individual member. Such a context comes from the organization, imagined as a whole, by its individual members. See Jean-Jacques Rousseau, *The Social Contract*, ed. Maurice Cranston (New York: Penguin Classics, 1961), book III, ch. 3.

11. John Rawls, *A Theory of Justice* (Cambridge, MA: Belknap Press, 1971), ch. 1, 3–53.

12. John Locke, *Second Treatise of Government*, in *Two Treatises of Government*, ed. Peter Laslett (New York: Cambridge University Press, 1991), chs. 7–9. Thomas Hobbes, *Leviathan*, ed. Edwin Curley (Indianapolis, IN: Hackett, 1994), ch. 13; "solitary, nasty, brutish and short" quote from 76.

13. While neither faced the lack of historical proof directly, each offered examples of continuing states of nature in non-European parts of the world and existing relations among sovereigns or nations. See Locke, *Second Treatise*, ch. 1, S14 and S15 and ch. 16, S184; and Hobbes, *Leviathan*, ch. 13, 11, and 12.

14. Origination requires consent. For Locke, the continued existence of government is implicitly consented to (Locke's term is *tacit consent*). See *Second Treatise*, ch. 8, S119. For Hobbes it is inherited as a result of the first irrevocable gift of powers to the leviathan. See note 17.

15. Locke, *Second Treatise*, chs. 7 and 8.

16. Locke, *Second Treatise*, ch. 5.

17. Hobbes, *Leviathan*, chs. 17 and 18.
See esp. 18 (XVIII "Of the Rights of Sovereigns by Institution"):

(1) A commonwealth is said to be instituted, when a multitude of men do agree and covenant, every one with every one, that to whatsoever man or assembly of men shall be given by the major part the right to present the person of them all (that is to say, to be their representative) every one, as well as he that voted for it as he that voted against it, shall authorize all the actions and judgments of that man or assembly of men, in the same manner as if they were his own, to the end, to live peaceably amongst themselves and be protected against other men.

(4) Because the right of bearing the person of them all is given to him they make sovereign by covenant only of one to another, and not of him to any of them, there can happen no breach of covenant on the part of the sovereign; and consequently none of his subjects, by any pretence of forfeiture, can be freed from his subjection. —Curley, ed. pp. 110 and 111.

18. Locke, *Second Treatise*, ch. 19.

19. See note 17.

20. Locke, *Second Treatise*, ch. 19, S220. "When the government is dissolved, the People are at liberty to provide for themselves, by erecting a new Legislative."

21. Hobbes, *Leviathan*, ch. 27 (3), "where laws ceaseth, sins ceaseth" and "when the sovereign power ceaseth, crime also ceaseth." Curley ed. p. 191.

22. Locke's *First Treatise* (in Laslett, *Two Treatises*) is a series of arguments against Robert Filmer's attempt to derive the right of kings from Adam.

23. For Locke, the first principle of natural law is that we not harm one another, and there is no evidence that he thought there was tremendous difficulty in obeying it. See *Second Treatise*, ch. III, S19, in which he describes the state of nature as "a State of Peace, good Will, Mutual Assistance, and Preservation." According to Hobbes, we are always at war with one another without government. See *Leviathan*, chs. 14 and 15.

24. Locke, *Second Treatise*, ch. 8, sec. 95–97, 330–32.

25. Although, of course, the degree of cooperation across party lines varies from administration to administration, depending on whether the president places a high value on building consensus, in addition to getting preferred programs approved by Congress. See, e.g., Ronald Brownstein, *The Second Civil War: How Extreme Partisanship Has Paralyzed Washington and Polarized America* (New York: Penguin Press, 2007).

26. Human life without all forms of government as we know them would probably be a subject for anthropology rather than political theory.

27. On the lasting effects of the earthquake in Pakistan see: Manabu and Kitagawa, "Asia: Winter Threatens to Compound Horror of Pakistani Earthquake," Asahi.com, December 17, 2005, at www.asahi.com and the European Parliament's 2007 analysis and assessment at http://www.europarl.europa.eu/sides/getDoc.do?Type=TA&Reference=P6-TA-2007-0214&language=EN.

28. In "Changing Homeland Security: The Issue-Attention Cycle," Christopher Bellavita discusses Anthony Downs's 1972 article "The Issue-Attention Cycle" (published in the summer issue of *Public Interest* 28), *Homeland Security Affairs* 1, no. 1, art. 1 (summer 2005), www.hsaj.org/?article=1.1.1.

29. For a comprehensive analysis of Locke's idea of private property and cooperative market economics in the state of nature, see C. B. MacPherson, *The Political Theory of Possessive Individualism*, Oxford, UK: Clarendon Press, 1962.

30. Locke, *Second Treatise*, ch. 7, S90. "For the end of Civil Society, being to avoid and remedy those inconveniencies of the State of Nature, which necessarily follow from every Man's being Judge in his own case."

31. If it seems as though I have posed and am now answering a straw man argument here, it should be remembered that even educated segments of the public tend to conflate individual failures within a system with the failure of the system as a

whole. Thus, for a recent example, after the global financial crisis in the fall of 2008, the academic publisher Karl-Dietz-Verlag reported an increase in sales of their edition of Karl Marx's *Das Kapital*. That increase, although it tripled 2007 sales, amounted to only one thousand more books sold; yet, the world press reported it as symptomatic of "a broader rejection of capitalism by many in eastern Germany." See Erik Kirschbaum, "Global Crisis Sends East Germans Flocking to Marx," Reuters, October 16, 2008, www.reuters.com/article/artsNews/idUSTRE49F5MX20081016.

32. Art Spiegelman, *In the Shadow of No Towers* (New York: Pantheon Books, 2004).

33. There was a very quick shift from an immediate post-9/11 pubic discussion of problems with American foreign policy that had garnered such evident hatred from radical Islamists to the broad view that criticism of the Bush administration was inadvisable, both because it was not yet known whether or how dissenters would be punished and because of the classic patriotism the attacks fostered. For discussion of these issues, see Joan Didion, *Fixed Ideas* (New York: New York Review of Books, 2003). Interestingly, in further support of Spiegelman's claim about the shift back to criticism-as-usual, in early 2007, the *New York Review of Books* was offering free copies of Didion's essay to new subscribers.

34. Spiegelman, *In the Shadow of No Towers*, 4.

35. However, according to Cary Nelson, current legal-activist president of the American Association of University Professors (AAUP) since 2001, the exclusion of foreign scholars based on the content of their work seems to have become a recent U.S. State Department policy. Though requirements for visas and entry to the United States had shifted to "conduct" instead of "content" after the end of the Cold War in the 1990s, they now seem in some cases to have shifted back again. It would be understandable if freedom of speech appeared less robust to scholars outside the United States than within it. The AAUP maintains up-to-date information on the status of specific cases on its website at www.aaup.org. See, e.g., "AAUP Challenges Ban on Foreign Scholar," AAUP, 2007, www.aaup.org/AAUP/newsroom/highlightsarchive/2007/Ramadan update.htm.

36. Apparently Bin Laden expected that only the tops of the towers would be destroyed. See "Bin Laden Surprised at Twin Tower Collapse," *Chicago Sun Times*, December 9, 2001, at www.highbeam.com/doc/1P2-4620305.html

37. *The 9/11 Commission Report: Final Report of the National Commission on Terrorist Attacks upon the United States*, 1st ed. (New York: W. W. Norton), 339–40. There is no date of publication listed in this edition. The 9/11 Commission was constituted by President George Bush on November 27, 2002, Public Law 107-306. The commission closed on August 21, 2007. The report is available online at www .9-11commission.gov.

38. *9/11 Commission Report*, 360.

39. *9/11 Commission Report*, 365.

5

Public Policy

Snakes on a Plane, Fire in the Pentagon, and Disaster Rights

SNAKES ON A PLANE AND FIRE IN THE PENTAGON

The 2006 movie *Snakes on a Plane* is a comic farce about contemporary air travel.[1] All of the characters are sufficiently foolish to deserve a good shaking up, but mainly the truly lewd, rude, gluttonous, or evil are ultimately punished. As in Jonathan Edwards's view of hell (discussed in chapter 2), a presumed virtuous audience is invited to enjoy the agonies of the damned. Such entertainment supports resistance to adequate disaster preparation and response in suggesting that only the bad are vulnerable.

Snakes on a Plane also popularizes what could prove to be an unwise national policy of treating safety and security as the same thing. Yes, a large number of aggressive and venomous snakes, unrestrained on a plane, would be unsafe. But so are metal fatigue and engine failure. The difference is that in the movie, correcting the snake situation is integrally related to finding out who perpetrated it and punishing these villains, whereas correcting the other problems does not require police action. (The snake criminals on the ground have to be apprehended immediately so that the correct antivenoms can be prepared for bites from different species of snakes.) We assume, perhaps rashly, that aging air-travel infrastructure has become a chronic condition for which no individual malefactors can be held responsible. But when the public perceives an acute danger, such as a terrorist attack or an anthrax outbreak, police action and safety procedures may be presented, perceived, and accepted as parts of the same appropriate response.[2]

I argued in chapter 1 that disaster-preparation planning is distinct from disaster-response planning and that moral principles should inform both. In chapter 4, I extended social contract theory to claim that government is

obligated to help those governed prepare for existence during the temporary absence of government. This obligation is based on the same principle
that justifies the founding of democratic government, namely, that government benefit those governed. Still, neither ethical insight about planning
nor fundamental government obligation theoretically derived constitutes a
practical program of disaster preparation and response. Public policy is the
necessary link between the ideals and abstractions of moral principle and
political obligation, on the one side, and what is actually done, on the other
side.

However, effective public policies with specific goals need to be justified
by more fundamental political commitments and understanding. In the
next two sections of this chapter, I consider the organization of the U.S. Department of Homeland Security (DHS) in terms of a now overlooked distinction between safety and security. The last two sections of the chapter
shift focus from the perspective of government officials and their actions to
the rights of disaster victims.

It should be emphasized that in our recent history, the conflation of issues of safety and security is rooted in the unpredicted physical attack on
national security when American Airlines Flight 77 struck the western fa-
cade of the Pentagon on September 11, 2001. In addition to 64 killed on
the aircraft, including the 5 terrorist hijackers, 125 Pentagon employees
died. A large area of the Pentagon, approximately eight hundred thousand
square feet, was demolished. In *Firefight*, Patrick Creed and Rick Newman
provide a comprehensive account of what happened on that day, putting
into historical perspective part of the national response to 9/11 that has incurred much criticism.[3] By noon on September 11, about three hours after
Flight 77 struck the Pentagon, the complex was simultaneously a major fire
scene, a medical treatment and triage area, an FBI crime scene, and the core
command center of ongoing U.S. government operations.

The intact side of the Pentagon housed the National Military Command
Center (NMCC), where the secretary of defense and his staff were working.
They were in contact with the president (who was on Air Force One), the
vice president (who was in a secure location beneath the White House), and
the North American Aerospace Defense Command in Cheyenne Mountain,
Colorado.[4] The NMCC and related personnel were able to continue their
operations during the days of the firefight at the Pentagon (rendered almost
unbearable by the need to contain a fire that had erupted between the at-
tics and roofs of the complex). But the terrorist attack on the national government was a physical reality that inevitably shaped the design of new administrative structures. It was the ultimate combination of breaches in
security and safety.

Still, even the terrorist aspect of the fire in the Pentagon did not make it
necessary to apprehend terrorists in dealing with that disaster. Rather, the

security breach was in the nature of the target (military headquarters and command center), as well as in the cause of the disaster (terrorist attack). The effects of Flight 77's crashing into the Pentagon were chaotic and destructive in ways reminiscent of a war zone for both firefighters and military personnel. But it was not literally a war zone, and one of the initial difficulties that firefighters had to contend with was the repeated attempts of military personnel to reenter the building to conduct their own rescue efforts.

Because the fire at the pentagon was a disaster and not an ongoing conflict, the Arlington County Fire Department, together with its partner departments from nearby areas, "owned" the location during the firefight. Neither the military nor the FBI had final say on what would be done at that fire scene. The Arlington fire chief handed over control of scene to the FBI on September 21, 2008.[5] The jurisdictional preeminence of the Arlington County Fire Department rested on its professional expertise for dealing with the crisis. Jurisdictional preeminence was not a matter of whose authority was at stake: the military almost lost its physical command center in the Pentagon when the plane crashed; by the morning of September 12, the fires on the roof of the Pentagon were threatening those parts of the complex that contained the heart of military communications[6]; before it took over the crime scene, the FBI deployed seven hundred of its agents to the site.

In reflecting on the 9/11 attack on the Pentagon, it is not easy to demarcate issues of safety from the security issues related to the cause of the disaster. The full events of 9/11 historically define contemporary (postmodern) terrorism as sudden, disastrous attacks against property and noncombatants. Terrorism is an assault on normal human activities, making it as much a social crime as a political and military one. The aim of terrorism is psychic as well as physical destruction because the disruption of ordinarily predictable life occasions the emotional attitude of terror in actual and potential victims. But because terror is an emotional response, a public climate of terror is not the best background for crisis assessment and planning. Even when leaders may not experience terror themselves, as some did on 9/11 at the Pentagon, the requirement that they do something very decisive in the wake of terrorist attacks may not result in the best choices of action.

HOMELAND SECURITY

For the foreseeable future, historians will likely describe the creation of the U.S. Department of Homeland Security as one of the political effects of the terrorist events of September 11, 2001. The creation of the DHS, which now includes the Federal Emergency Management Agency (FEMA), is a concrete example of public policy for disaster. Here is a rough outline of how this new system is supposed to work. There is the National Response Plan (NRP), according to which the secretary of DHS is the president's main disaster advisor. Advice from the DHS secretary can enable the president to use his or her authority under the Stafford Act to direct federal agencies, such as the Departments of Defense and Health and Human Services, to respond to a threat to homeland security or a catastrophe. The 1988 Stafford Act (an amendment to the 1974 version) authorizes the president to bypass normal states' rights by declaring a disaster and marshalling federal resources for aid.[7] As the president's disaster advisor, the secretary of DHS designates an event an Incident of National Significance and further has the authority to convene the Interagency Incident Management Group, designate a principle federal official, and invoke the NRP's Catastrophic Incident Annex (NPR-CIA). NPR-CIA applies mainly to short- or no-notice events, and its invocation shifts the federal response from a reaction to requests from states, or a "pull" system, to proactive measures, or a "push" system. That was the system in place when Hurricane Katrina occurred.

DHS AND HURRICANE KATRINA

Concerning Hurricane Katrina, a 2006 bipartisan report by the U.S. House of Representatives claimed that the Secretary of DHS executed the responsibilities of the department "late, ineffectively, or not at all." Although the head of FEMA used a "push" model in the field, the Secretary did not officially invoke NPR-CIA, and the White House Homeland Security Council, as the operating head of DHS, failed to analyze varied damage assessments and to consider an eyewitness account of a levee breach as "confirmed" for eleven hours. It's safe to say that from many perspectives, the DHS response to Hurricane Katrina was unsatisfactory.[8] It is impossible to determine whether this was mainly the result of DHS's organization, or of its newness, or of other factors such as inadequate preparation. It seems safe to say, however, that DHS's organization had something to do with what was unsatisfactory about the response to Hurricane Katrina.

SAFETY

The creation of the Department of Homeland Security initially tied it to the prevention of more terrorist attacks within the United States after 9/11: the "homeland" would be "secured." The effects of terrorist attacks are only one kind of disaster, and "security" understood as protection from human enemies is not the same thing as *safety*. Safety is a more general concern than security because safety requires prudent protection from all probable dangers, whereas *security* is protection from dangers arising from the illegal aggression of others. All breaches of security are unsafe, whereas not all unsafe conditions or events are breaches of security. For example, the eruption of a volcano is unsafe, but it is not in itself a security problem. Some breaches of safety may become security issues. (If your front door falls off its hinges due to faulty construction, your house may be more vulnerable to burglars.) But when something is primarily a security issue, it involves the illegal intentions of human beings and requires a special focus to correct. Such correction goes beyond a preservation of safety, although it would also be unsafe not to correct it.

Terrorism is, of course, unsafe, but what constitutes its condition of not being safe is different from how it violates security. It is the difference between someone throwing a large rock through your bedroom window and the wind blowing the panes out, between identity thieves and raccoons going through your desk drawers. This difference comes down to the absence or presence of human ill will. Floods can be caused by criminal explosions, and fires may be caused by arsonists, but in such disasters, the presence of FEMA, as a part of Homeland Security, is not to apprehend such perpetrators but to restore the public safety disrupted by the disasters themselves. In their post-Katrina compendium, *Disasters and the Law*, Daniel Farber and Jim Chen state the problem of the conflation of security with safety in terms of practical policy:

> Nearly four years after September 11, 2001, Katrina posed the question as coarsely as possible: did the United States fundamentally err in assigning responsibility for all emergency response, including relief and rebuilding efforts in connection with natural disasters, to an agency whose principle mission is directed toward detecting and preventing terrorist attacks?[9]

Farber and Chen go on to cite evidence from cognitive psychology that the confusion of safety with security is a "natural" human error: human beings in general tend to posit living agents, such as other humans, animals, or "anthropomorphic deities," as causes in preference to inanimate objects or natural forces. Humans tend to fear events with low probabilities and great danger, compared to more ordinary or constant risks. Risk is often calculated according to how easy it is to imagine an example, and the strength of a response to an event is directly related to its vividness. Also, widespread instances of "probability neglect" lead to a focus on what has emotional effects rather than actual probabilities. For example, a mistaken and overly emotional evaluation of risk led millions of Americans to drive instead of fly after 9/11, which is estimated to have caused about 353 additional deaths between September 11 and December 31, 2001.[10] Based on this research, Farber and Chen raise an empirical psychological question about how safety may have become conflated with security after 9/11: "To what extent does the entire system of emergency response, especially insofar as this body of law was developed in the immediate aftermath of September 11, reflect a collective exercise in the mistaken evaluation of risk?"[11]

The DHS has from its inception been politicized in ways that may distort the most broad and general practical requirements of a safety program. Safety is a matter of what will be done for people and what they should do themselves; its overall purpose is not the apprehension and punishment of those who have violated security or might do so—even though dealing with security violators might be a special safety function requiring the activation of state or federal investigators and police or military. The appeal in the popular imagination of viewing safety and security as the same thing is like the appeal of viewing disaster preparation and prevention as the same thing: authorities can be viewed as ultimate moral protectors, who apprehend evildoers and assure the public's safety in the same action(s). Thus, when an evildoer is known to be responsible, it's only necessary to remove that person to stop his or her crimes. But we now know that in decentralized, multigenerational, contemporary terrorism, it is not that simple. Much less does any criminal-apprehension model address the effects of natural catastrophe.

Not only is the conflation of security and safety similar to the conflation of prevention and preparation, but it promotes overlooking preparation toward an almost total focus on response. Safety is largely a matter of preparation, whereas security concentrates on response to known danger. The mindset of security response, to the exclusion of safety preparation, has come to dominate popular views of disaster. This perspective continually leaves us with merely retrospective analyses and regret for the fates of victims.

The subsumption of safety under security on an organizational level may privilege issues of security over safety, even though neglect of safety issues could result in greater destruction and human harm. In *Introduction to Emergency Management*, George Haddow and Jane Bullock describe the transition from an *all-hazards* approach to disaster to a terrorist-centered one after 9/11 as follows: "In the new Department of Homeland Security (DHS), FEMA becomes a division headed by an Undersecretary that reports up through a Deputy Secretary to the Department Secretary." The authors go on to predict diminished organizational stature for the head of FEMA, competition for resources with DHS, and the deflection of federal funds not needed for counterterrorist activities to budget shortfall purposes on the level of state government.[12] Haddow and Bullock liken the post-9/11 focus on terrorism to FEMA's concentration of 75 percent of its resources on nuclear-war preparation during the 1980s. The result of that was diminished ability to deal with the natural catastrophes of a series of hurricanes: Hugo, Iniki, and Andrew.[13]

Farber and Chen highlight two significant types of proposed policy reform following DHS's performance during Hurricane Katrina. The first, based partly on President Calvin Coolidge's response to the 1927 Mississippi River flood, advocates a new cabinet-level "disaster-response czar." The second, in a report by the Senate Committee on Homeland Security and Government Affairs, advocates the abolition of FEMA and a new National Preparedness and Response Authority (NPRA) within DHS.[14] However, the problem is probably less an issue of organizational structure than of what a disaster-response czar, or the replacement of FEMA, or even DHS and FEMA as presently organized will perceive as the primary mission, safety or security.[15] Safety and security share the goal of protecting the government, the country, and the people. But the expertise and methods for protection are obviously different in each case. We could say that although government is involved administratively in safety, safety is primarily a civilian issue. Security, with government involvement beyond administration, which includes surveillance, apprehension, and punishment, is more of a police/military matter. Safety policies and procedures require broad publicity and transparency to be effective, whereas security requires a degree of secrecy.

If the recent past is a lesson, organizational issues will continually be resolved and revised as new disasters occur until the public becomes sufficiently aware of the value of safety and preparation. Moreover, given the complexity of contemporary life and government, even the best organization models will unavoidably have messy overlaps, which need not impair the effectiveness of either safety or security missions. For example, the U.S. Department of Defense has traditionally been responsible for flood control and the oversight of ocean resources and oil reserves, and the Bureau of Alcohol, Tobacco, Firearms, and Explosives is a law-enforcement agency that is part of the Department of the Treasury. It is important that any conflation in organizational structures between safety and security not be such that the primary goals of either, as well as the general goal of protection, are obstructed.

Even ideally constructed security-response and safety-preparation programs, together with the most efficient government procedures, will not *guarantee* safety in dangerous times. Unpredictable, as well as predictable but unpredicted, disastrous events will occur, and that contingency will continually put the spotlight on response. We are perpetually caught between the task of preparing for predictable disasters and guessing at responses to those unprepared for. Restraint and conscientiousness are necessary to continue to prepare for predictable dangers, despite the more spectacular nature of the unpredictable ones and the genuine heroism evoked in response to them.

DISASTER RIGHTS AND AIRLINE PASSENGERS' RIGHTS

If, toward satisfactory disaster preparation and response, the obligations of government are recognized, certain moral ideals are accepted, and there is a clear and effective public policy for safety, then that combination should be sufficient to optimize human life and well-being in principled ways. However, the combination may not be sufficient for two reasons. First, government obligations, moral ideals, and effective safety policy all concern the actions of officials. Although the subject, or "patient," for officials includes private individuals and the pubic en masse, this subject is only considered as it is affected by what officials do. And second, the combination might be fulfilled, but in unforeseen circumstances, the well-being of individuals may not be maximized because their dignity is violated, their preferences, aversions, and differences are ignored, or their normal life commitments are unnecessarily disregarded. One way to focus on individuals in anticipation of disaster and to keep them informed as individuals would be to compose, promulgate, and respect *disaster rights*. That is, the politics, moral ideals, and public policies for disaster, taken together, might still need to be supplemented with an idea of human rights as they apply to disaster, or possibly new rights for disaster.

It may seem redundant to add human rights to the other moral and practical requirements and constraints of disaster. But if it is redundant, it will leave the rest of the combination intact, and no harm will be done. If disaster rights address issues not covered by the combination of political obligations, moral ideals, and public policy, then their addition will be beneficial. There is, however, the theoretical problem that human rights are assumed to be universal, to cover all people in all situations. Nevertheless, there are precedents for specialized rights. Consumers, patients, and, most recently, airline passengers have recognized rights based on distinctive circumstances. If we can talk seriously about an Airline Passenger's Bill of Rights—and the Senate Commerce Committee has—then disaster, which is a more general, and more dangerous, human condition than air travel, could generate special rights.

Let's consider the circumstances under which the demand for an Airline Passengers' Bill of Rights arose and the nature of those rights. In December 2006, American Airlines passengers flying from San Francisco to Dallas were diverted to Austin because of storms in Dallas. The passengers were kept in planes on the tarmacs for over eight hours without working bathrooms, food, or fresh water. The Coalition for an Airline Passengers Bill of

Rights was formed, spearheaded by Kate Hanni, who expressed their position as follows: "Now we are saying enough is enough. The basic tenet . . . is that we want the airlines to have our well-being at interest. We want to know that our best interest is at stake ultimately and that never again is anyone left in the place where we were left."[16] The coalition, with the support of the U.S. Public Interest Research Group, prompted the Senate Commerce Committee to approve a Federal Aviation Administration (FAA) reauthorization bill on May 16, 2007, which included passenger-rights language (sponsored by Senators Barbara Boxer [D-CA] and Olympia Snowe [R-ME]). (Finalization still requires action by the House Transportation Committee in conjunction with FAA reauthorization legislation, passage by the House, and presidential signing into law.)

The main parts of an Airline Passengers' Bill of Rights are taken to include procedures for deplaning passengers stuck in planes on tarmacs for over three hours, provision of essential needs for passengers during any delay onboard, truthful reporting of flight delays and cancellations, and return of diverted luggage within twenty-four hours. The Coalition for an Airline Passengers' Bill of Rights has also complained that the Department of Transportation has failed to accurately report extended delays on diverted flights, as well as travel delays or interruptions due to cancelled flights.[17]

The rights at stake here boil down to comfort for passengers, access to accurate accounts of their immediate travel situation, and property rights. Not everyone can afford to fly, and flying is to a large extent optional. It therefore might seem as though airline passenger rights, compared to more general human rights, are matters of convenience rather than necessity. However, to the extent that in normal times our survival derives from our livelihoods, and many jobs require air travel, passenger rights are not frivolous. And nonbusiness travelers would seem to share the same right of unobstructed movement to pursue leisure activities, such as education, medical care, vacations, hobbies, or visits with friends and relatives. Neither are passengers' concerns about their property and respect for their property rights in their baggage unusual, given the overall importance of private property rights in U.S. society. Passengers do not willingly accept the discomfort attending their present treatment by the airlines whenever they buy plane tickets. The amount of discomfort that can simply be inflicted on passengers would be negotiable if passengers could be viewed as an organized interest group, which they cannot without recognized rights as such. In this sense, the granting of a bill of rights for airline passengers would not only create their rights as airline passengers but at the same time recognize them as a distinct group with a political voice. It's not clear that such recognition is necessary, insofar as any reasonable airline passengers' bill of rights would boil down to respect for persons, freedom of movement, and property rights, all of which are already recognized as unexceptionable, basic human rights.

Either in creating new rights or reinforcing old ones in new situations, the Airline Passengers' Bill of Rights would bring attention to the violation of existing human rights in situations not specifically covered by traditional rights doctrines. Current abuses indicate that such attention is necessary in the case of air travel. Would it not be even more necessary in the case of disaster, given known abuses in recent times? Before going further with this idea, it would be helpful to consider human rights in the normal sense.

NORMAL HUMAN RIGHTS

Rights are freedoms *from* certain things (i.e., protections), as well as freedoms *for* other things (i.e., liberties). Rights concern human interactions and generate principles or rules of action; rights are deontological (see chapter 2). Questions concerning disaster rights would include, What protections and liberties are inviolable, sacrosanct? What should not be allowed to happen to people in disasters? What should people not be prevented from, or supported in, doing during disasters?" Even provisional answers to those questions could suggest very specific legal and administrative changes from the present situation. However, it is not easy to articulate a bill of rights for disaster that both has the moral content acceptable in a democratic society and avoids the self-defeating, narrow, political disagreement that accompanies evocation of the "philosophical principles" of political parties.

The idea of disaster rights comes up against the same kind of broad political disagreement that informs so much of contemporary political debate in the United States: in relation to government, are rights fundamentally *safeguards* to protect citizens against the abuse of government power, or are rights *entitlements*? The safeguard view of rights is evident in the preamble to the Bill of Rights, which comprises the U.S. Constitution's first ten amendments: "The Conventions of a number of the States, having at the time of their adopting the Constitution, expressed a desire, in order to prevent misconstruction or abuse of its powers, that further declaratory and restrictive clauses should be added."[18] Similarly, the English Bill of Rights of 1689, called "An Act Declaring the Rights and Liberties of the Subject and Settling the Succession of the Crown," begins with a list of abuses of the freedom of citizens and restrictions on parliamentary elections committed by King James II.[19] By contrast, rights as entitlements are evident in the French, Norwegian, German, and Latin American legal systems, which assign positive duties of assistance and care to government.[20] Americans have, of course, accepted entitlements in pension, welfare, and medical care, but not with stable guarantees—the future of even Social Security is at times uncertain—and not as rights.

The UN Declaration of Human Rights promulgates universal rights as both safeguards and entitlements. Articles 1 and 2 assert universal human equality with regard to rights and freedoms. Articles 3 to 13 assert individual human liberties and rights to life and personal safety. Articles 14 to 21 assert basic political rights and liberties. Articles 22 to 28 assert what in the U.S. context would be considered "entitlements." Mentioned in Articles 22 to 28 are rights to individual development, fair employment, education, social security, cultural participation, and an adequate standard of living. Article 25 is noteworthy for claiming security for the ill, unemployed, and disabled, as well as special entitlements for mothers and children. Article 29 asserts the duties of individuals to their communities, according to their capabilities. Article 30 claims that nothing in the declaration implies that any individual or group may violate the foregoing rights and freedoms, and it thereby removes the distinction between listed rights and entitlements from the UN perspective.

DISASTER RIGHTS

Several points relevant to disaster emerge from the foregoing discussions of rights. In the American legal tradition, rights have generally been asserted on behalf of citizens against government. That tradition is grounds to assume that disaster rights would also entail the rights of citizens or other residents against government and governmental authority. One reason for developing and promulgating distinctive disaster rights is that ordinary protections and freedoms may not be sufficiently safeguarded in disasters. If unpredictable and urgent conditions require a suspension of ordinary rights, the question is, Does the situation of rights suspension itself need a distinctive set of rights? In other words, if government changes its fundamental policies, are new rights necessary?

In the U.S. Constitution, the Bill of Rights does not shape, but rather provides a check on, the U.S. government as it is described in the Constitution. On that basis, we could not say that disaster rights will either shape what the government does in disaster or determine the form of a sufficiently different government that might arise to deal with disaster. We could say that any form of government that does exist during disaster might be constrained by some rights. All rights cannot be suspended in imaginable disasters because if that were the case, then anyone or everyone could be arbitrarily killed by the government, and the government itself would be illegal. So, what rights may not be suspended? One absolute right would be the right to life of innocent individuals. The absolute right of innocent individuals to their lives seems morally self-evident to many, but as we shall see later, in the European dignitarian tradition, which posits an intrinsic worth of the human individual, innocents' right to life is absolute in legal terms.

Given political tensions between rights as safeguards and rights as entitlements, it is probably either unrealistic or opportunistic to use situations of disaster to introduce entitlements that would not be expected in normal times. This is tricky, however, because without normal livelihood or access to customary necessities, assistance itself may resemble an entitlement more than a right. However, if assistance is based on a prior governmental social contract obligation to make life better for those governed—as argued in chapter 4—then assistance becomes a right. The question is, How much better should government make life during a disaster; that is, how much assistance is government obligated to provide? In life-and-death emergency conditions, citizens have an absolute right to survival assistance. But in recovery phases, free market forces may take over, and government assistance will be resisted on the grounds that it is an entitlement.

Suppose that government ought to do everything possible in disasters to preserve those rights that are recognized in normal times. This would mean that freedom of speech, belief, and assembly, as well as privacy rights and due process, would all be presumed to continue intact unless their protection endangered the more primary right to life. A second important operating principle is that such rights be preserved without discrimination or bias on the basis of any social factor according to which it is unacceptable for the government to discriminate in normal times. However, to the degree that social disadvantage due to race, class, physical ability, age, and gender is already institutionalized prior to a disaster, if nothing else is done, the realities of disaster itself will have discriminatory effects. (Such effects will be addressed in chapter 6.)

The American legal tradition holds that the government must protect rights to property ownership but not that it is obligated to repair damaged private property. But property repair may be necessary for survival in a disaster. This looks like an entitlement but could be explained as fulfillment of the social contract obligation. By the same token, it may be necessary in some conditions of disaster that government destroy or reallocate private property so that a greater number can survive. Also, survival may require that individuals abandon substantial amounts of their personal property in addition to their real estate. It is therefore difficult to see how normal property rights can be sustained in disasters without qualification.

Disasters typically result in the sudden destruction of significant amounts of property. Government already recognizes a responsibility to mitigate such effects (e.g., to build levees that will withstand storm surges of a preagreed level)[21] and to compensate victims after the fact (e.g., FEMA's underwriting of private insurance policies).[22] However, government protection of property rights, like property rights themselves, is meaningful only in a prior social and political context that sustains possession and use. If an entire neighborhood and the infrastructure of a city are destroyed in a disaster, as happened in New Orleans after Hurricane Katrina, the fact that government action could have prevented that destruction does not entail a violation of the property rights of those who do not return home because they cannot count on schools, hospitals, employment, or the return of other residents.[23] Frustration, rage, and grief due to such loss is both understandable and rationally justified, but it cannot be used as an argument for stronger property rights than the contextualized nature of property rights admits. At the conclusion of a bleak analysis of the financial, technological, and geological problems attending a restoration of New Orleans, Kenneth Foster and Robert Giegengack observe the following:

> The United States has not been accustomed to planning for events that would result in the physical or economic loss of a city. But cities have been lost repeatedly in the past. We need only consider the history of such ancient cities as Pompeii, Tikal, Knossos, Machu Picchu, Leptis Magna, or Santorini—the list goes on—to realize that major cities have been destroyed by natural processes in the past, and the societies that made those cities the cultural beacons they became moved their cities elsewhere.[24]

Moving a city is not the same thing as rebuilding. Moreover, how are the inhabitants to know when it is time to move their city collectively? The historical record of cities passing into oblivion sounds lame, given the frustration, grief, and rage recognized earlier. That is because a rights-based approach to disaster response, including recovery, is inherently limited in a legal system that confines rights to restrictions on government. The most powerful contribution of government to citizen and resident well-being in disaster lies in fulfilling its obligation to justify its existence according to social contract theory (as discussed in chapter 4). Rights may come into play in immediate official responses to disaster, but preparation for disaster during normal times is where and when government can fulfill its core obligation to make life better for those governed. Demands for the fulfillment of that obligation are also best made in normal times through the exercise of the normal rights of free speech, assembly, and voting.

DIGNITY AND DISASTER VICTIMS

In his *Metaphysical Principles of Virtue*, originally published in 1797, Emmanuel Kant distinguishes between human beings as persons having intrinsic value, or as ends in themselves, and all other things, including man viewed as a mere animal or commodity:

> Man in the system of nature (homo phaenomenon, animal rationale) is a being of little significance and, along with the other animals, considered as products of

the earth, has an ordinary value. . . . But man as a person, i.e., as the subject of a morally-practical reason, is exalted above all price. For such a one (homo noumenon) he is not to be valued merely as a means to the ends of other people, or even to his own ends, but is to be prized as an end in himself. This is to say, he possesses a dignity (an absolute inner worth) whereby he exacts the respect of all other rational beings in the world, can measure himself against each member of his species, and can esteem himself on a footing of equality with them.[25]

Kant compares human skills that can be priced and the value of human preferences. But the sense in which persons are ends in themselves and not means to other ends is precisely their unpriceable dignity:

Whatever has reference to general human inclinations and needs has a market price; whatever, without presupposing any need, accords with a certain taste, i.e., a delight in the mere unpurposive play of our mental powers, has an effective price; but that which constitutes the condition under which alone something can be an end in itself has not merely a relative worth, i.e., a price, but has an intrinsic worth, i.e., dignity.[26]

Despite this elevated prose, Kant restricted his idea of universal human dignity to those he considered "persons," namely, rational, racially white, European males.[27] Not until the twentieth century was it taken for granted that all human beings are persons. Moreover, doctrines about human rights did not focus on, or proceed from, a moral idea of dignity in Kant's sense of "absolute inner worth" until they were incorporated into new founding documents during the twentieth century. Mary Glendon, in her account of how Eleanor Roosevelt led the United Nations Commission, which produced the Universal Declaration of Human Rights, notes that after World War II, most new constitutions and treaties were *dignitarian*. For example, the German Basic Law of 1949 begins in Article I, "The dignity of man shall be inviolable. To respect and protect it shall be the duty of all state authority."[28] And the preamble to the UN Declaration of Human Rights (published on December 10, 1948) begins, "WHEREAS recognition of the inherent dignity and of the equal and inalienable rights of all members of the human family is the foundation of freedom, justice and peace in the world."[29]

When passengers are kept on airplanes for many hours without being informed of when they will be in flight, the interruption of their plans and accompanying physical discomfort may not be a violation of their fundamental legal rights, but it is an affront to their dignity. When disaster victims are herded together like cattle, separated from family members, and left for days without the basics of survival in conditions without facilities for personal hygiene or privacy, it is a more serious affront to their dignity.

An affront to dignity is not the same as a violation of dignity in a core sense, but human dignity has trappings, such as ease of movement, respect for the human physical body, and minimal comfort. Once these trappings are removed, more fundamental respect for persons in that situation may no longer seem to be as stringently required. When people are confined, deprived, disheveled, and dirty, they may be objects of pity and concern, but respect is not going to be a primary attitude in responding to them.[30] If respect for human dignity is a precondition for freedom, justice, and peace, as claimed in the UN declaration, then universal human dignity ought to be assumed and respected in thinking about the rights of disaster victims. Everything that may be merely uncomfortable and inconvenient in airplane delays becomes dangerous in disaster. The relation of respect to apparent social status may cash out cruelly in violations of dignity when, for example, disaster victims lose real foundations of social status, such as their homes and personal property.

As noted in the European rights tradition and the UN Declaration of Universal Rights, recognition of the dignity of individuals is presumed to be a primary political principle. Dignity is affirmed, and both safeguards against government and entitlements to economic, developmental, and social well-being are presented as following from the recognition of dignity. Human dignity is a moral value. If its recognition is the foundation of all government action (as claimed in the German Basic Law) in the dignitarian tradition, then, as in the social contract tradition, morality is the foundation and justification of legitimate government.

The European dignitarian tradition is based on the absolute worth of individual human life as an *intrinsic* value, that is, a value contained within itself and for itself. This value is the foundation for human rights in ways that often find direct expression in laws. For example, the German constitution, or Basic Law, has been interpreted not to permit compliance with the U.S. Aviation Security Law adopted after 9/11, which permits military destruction of aircraft with civilian passengers that have been taken over by terrorists. That is, according to the Basic Law, because human dignity is absolute and inviolable, it cannot be measured so that a smaller number may be sacrificed to save a larger number.[31]

In the United States, respect for human dignity occurs more as a moral intuition than an explicit component of laws. A large part of the public outrage at the delay in assistance to the victims of Hurricane Katrina was an unspoken sense that their dignity as individuals had been violated. Part of the violation was based on the fact that in an affluent and technologically advanced society, supplies and services should have been more quickly available. In a poor and technologically challenged society, these conditions might not have been experienced by the Katrina victims, and perceived by their observers, as a violation of dignity. This suggests that although dignity, in the sense of intrinsic worth, is absolute, what violates it is relative. It also suggests that citizens and residents have an absolute right not to have their dignity violated in disasters.

The absolute rights of disaster victims that can be defended in the American legal tradition are few: right to innocent life, right to assistance in emergencies, and only perhaps, *if they can get it*, right to respect for individual dignity. Nevertheless, observers respond with great compassion to those who suffer in disasters, especially if their rights have been violated or their dignity not recognized and preserved. Some of that humanitarian response is extended to members of disadvantaged groups, who might otherwise be refused assistance in normal times because they are generally believed not to have earned, or otherwise *deserve*, it. The situation of the disadvantaged in contemporary American disasters will be the subject of chapter 6. It should be noted here that the return to humanitarian compassion is a compromise in light of stronger social contract obligations of government to assist citizens in disaster preparation (see chapter 4). It could be argued that when the more primary social contract obligation has not been fulfilled, it incurs a compensatory obligation to make up for that in response so that government is required to respond in extraordinary ways if it has not fulfilled its social contract obligations of preparation. But before that could be carried out, the more fundamental social contract obligation would have to be widely recognized. Without such recognition, we are indeed back to the humanitarian aspects of response. Still, given the importance of human dignity in the European political tradition after World War II, this is no small thing.

NOTES

1. In case the reader has not seen the movie—indeed, I would not expect it of many readers, here is the plot. A surfer, Sean Jones (Nathan Phillips), witnesses the murder of a prosecutor by Eddie Kim (Byron Lawson) and his accomplices. Sean is taken under the wing of FBI agent Neville Flynn (Samuel L. Jackson) so that he will live to testify against Kim. They get on a Boeing 747 from Honolulu to Los Angeles. But Kim has arranged for the storage in the plane's cargo hold of a number of crates of venomous snakes, which will be opened by automatic timers. The snakes are primed to become extremely aggressive when they smell the pheromones sprayed onto the leis distributed to the passengers in Honolulu. A couple having sex in the bathroom are the first gory casualties, and it's downhill from there, in scenes combining the best and worst of the *Alien* and *Top Gun* movies. Another passenger is killed in the toilet when a snake latches onto his penis. An obese woman is encircled by snakes that have slid under her clothing. One of two children flying alone for the first time is cruelly bitten. An obnoxious passenger tries to pacify a python by flinging the little yappy dog of Mercedes (Rachel Blanchard), a spoiled rich woman, into its mouth, and in time, the python satisfyingly makes a meal of him

too. Flynn's partner, the pilot, and the copilot, as well as a sympathetic elderly stewardess on the brink of retirement, are all slain.

Mercedes saves all who have survived up to a point by sending herpetologist Steven Price (Todd Louiso) photos of the dead snakes with her smartphone so that he can procure antivenom medication for the survivors if and when they land. Meanwhile, after the passengers have built futile luggage barricades, Flynn shoots out two of the plane's windows to suck out the snakes, delivering the line subsequently said to have flown around the Internet: "Enough is enough! I have had it with these motherfucking snakes on this motherfucking plane!" Flynn now has to take the controls of the plane under the directions of Troy, one of the bodyguards of passenger rapper Three Gs. Troy has had two thousand hours' flight experience. But (shades of *The Phoenix*) it turns out that Troy's experience was from a flight simulator for PlayStation 2! No matter—they land safely, the good guys get date promises from the attractive stewardesses, and the bad guys are tracked down and killed. In the final scene, Sean Jones is shown surfing with Neville Flynn, presumably in Bali, where he had been planning to go before witnessing the prosecutor's murder.

2. See, e.g., Bill McGee, "Focus on Terrorism May Obscure Other Airline Safety Threats," *USA Today*, October 3, 2007, www.usatoday.com/travel/columnist/mcgee/2007-10-03-airline-safety-threats_N.htm.

3. Patrick Creed and Rick Newman, *Firefight: Inside the Battle to Save the Pentagon on 9/11* (New York: Ballantine Books, 2008).

4. Creed and Newman, *Firefight*, 171–72, 177 ff.

5. However, the fire fighters had to reassert this authority continually. See, e.g., Creed and Newman, *Firefight*, 143–44, 244–51.

6. Creed and Newman, *Firefight*, 316–17.

7. See www.fema.gov/about/stafact.shtm.

8. The structural description and quotation are from *Final Report of the Select Bipartisan Committee to Investigate the Preparation for and Response to Hurricane Katrina*, in Daniel A. Farber and Jim Chen, *Disasters and the Law: Katrina and Beyond* (New York: Aspen Publishers, 2006), 69–70.

9. Farber and Chen, *Disasters and the Law*, 71.

10. Farber and Chen, *Disasters and the Law*, 71–72.

11. Farber and Chen, *Disasters and the Law*, 72.

12. George D. Haddow and Jane A. Bullock, *Introduction to Emergency Management* (Burlington, MA: Elsevier Science, 2003), 239.

13. Haddow and Bullock, *Introduction to Emergency Management*, 242.

14. See "Reforming the Law of Disaster Response," in Haddow and Bullock, *Introduction to Emergency Management*, 93–108.

15. On the U.S. cabinet departments, see www.whitehouse.gov/government/cabinet.html.

16. See www.bizjournals.com/dallas/stories/2007/o1/22/daily20.html.

17. This information and further updates are available at http://strandedpassengers.blogsport.com and also on the U.S. PIRG website at www.uspirg.org.

18. See www.archives.gov/exhibits/charters/bill_of_rights.html.

19. See www.webmesh.co.uk/englishbillofrights1689.htm.

20. Cf. Mary Ann Glendon, *A World Made New: Eleanor Roosevelt and the Universal Declaration of Human Rights* (New York: Random House, 2001), xvii.

21. On both the assessments and decisions that resulted in the pre-Katrina levee capabilities and for a model of a more democratic decision procedure, see Detlof Von Winterfeldt, "Using Risk and Decision Analysis to Protect New Orleans against Future Hurricanes," in *On Risk and Disaster: Lessons from Hurricane Katrina,* ed. Ronald J. Daniels, Donald F. Kent, and Howard Kunreuther (Philadelphia: University of Pennsylvania Press, 2006), 27–40.

22. On the difficult situation facing individual home owners after Katrina, see Peter G. Gosselin, "On Their Own in Battered New Orleans," in Daniels, Kent, and Kunreuther, *On Risk and Disaster,* 15–26.

23. Rep. Richard J. Baker (R-LA), chairman of a House financial-market subcommittee, commented, "What's missed is that it wasn't a single house or business that was destroyed, but an entire region. . . . It does no good to stand up just one person or family, because there's nothing left where they once lived—no schools or grocery stores, doctors or banks, police stations or fire trucks." Daniels, Kent, and Kunreuther, *On Risk and Disaster,* 17.

24. Kenneth R. Foster and Robert Giegengack, "Planning for a City on the Brink," in Daniels, Kent, and Kunreuther, *On Risk and Disaster,* 41–58. Quote is from 56–57.

25. Emmanuel Kant, *Metaphysical Principles of Virtue,* in *Emmanuel Kant, Ethical Philosophy,* trans. James W. Ellington (Indianapolis, IN: Hackett, 1994), ch. 2, 97. Also at praxeology.net/kant8.htm.

26. Emmanuel Kant, *Grounding for the Metaphysics of Morals,* Second Section, in Ellington, trans., *Emmanuel Kant, Ethical Philosophy,* 40.

27. See Naomi Zack, *Philosophy of Science and Race* (New York: Routledge, 2002), ch. 1.

28. Glendon, *A World Made New,* 263n2.

29. Glendon, *A World Made New,* 310; also at www.un.org/Overview/rights.html.

30. This is no more than a commonsense observation, although it's often overlooked. Service personnel in all venues reserve their best treatment for people who are well groomed and well dressed, compared to those who look poor and sloppy. The homeless are often bared from entry into retail establishments based on their appearance alone, regardless of whether they have money. Racial minorities work against the same lack of respect based on their appearance, although in this case, social status in public places is not only linked to evident wealth or self-care but to unchangeable signs of devalued racial or ethnic identity.

31. See Raymond Youngs, "Germany: Shooting Down Aircraft and Analyzing Computer Data," *International Journal of Constitutional Law* 6, no. 2 (2008): 331–48; abstract at http://icon.oxfordjournals.org/egi/content/abstract/6/2/331.

6

The Disadvantaged and Disaster

Hurricane Katrina

SHAME

We are a society that treats human remains with respect. In wartime, the dead are transported home and buried with great solemnity, attended by friends, relatives, neighbors, and public dignitaries. The flags that drape their coffins are ceremoniously folded and reverently handed to spouses, parents, or children. In the days after the Twin Towers of the World Trade Center collapsed, New York City Fire Department personnel worked around the clock, forming brigades to carefully bring out containers of human remains. During the firefight at the Pentagon, the FBI meticulously oversaw the search for, and retrieval, documentation, and transportation of, human remains. The remains ranged in size from tissue measured in inches to intact corpses. Each set of remains was carried out of the Pentagon by at least two members of the Old Guard elite ceremonial unit from Fort Myers, who were escorted into and out of the Pentagon for that purpose by Federal Emergency Management Agency (FEMA) officials. Great care was taken to avoid media and Internet spectacles of "body parts."[1] Official efforts of this nature are intended to protect human dignity, as well as to honor those who died while serving their country.

For days after Hurricane Katrina, the world continually viewed Ethel Freeman's body in her wheelchair at the Superdome. Corpses floating face down in floodwater or left to bloat on the streets of New Orleans were visible on hundreds of millions of computer and television screens. These images violated human dignity.

In his 1964 protest song "The Lonesome Death of Hattie Carroll,"[2] Bob Dylan sings a refrain to "you who philosophize disgrace and criticize all fears," which cautions as the story unfolds, "Now ain't the time for your tears." The song is based on a true story. William Zantzinger (the "t" is left out of his name in the song), a twenty-four-year-old son of white Southern landowners, killed Hattie Carroll, fifty years old and black, a hotel kitchen worker and mother of ten, by slinging his cane at her across a room. Zantzinger was arrested, released on bail, convicted by an all-white jury, and sentenced by the judge.[3] After Dylan recounts that Zantzinger got a sentence of six months, he ends, "Now's the time for your tears."

The overt, violent racism that Dylan and others exposed to public view during the civil rights movement is no longer morally acceptable in its communities of origin. But terrible violations of human dignity continue to happen to black people in the United States, during normal life as well as disaster. These affronts, and the pain and grief they cause, are ameliorated, but not expunged, by the fact that most whites would not now deliberately inflict them or tolerate those who do. When blacks, but not whites, suffer such affronts, the general evil of the widespread, intentional racism of the past is *evoked*.

In every civilian disaster thus far, the already disadvantaged have suffered most, and there is little doubt that this will continue to be the case. Legal and political arguments for preventing that continuity are not likely to be immediately effective. Neither moral argument nor cultural criticism is decisive, but both are worth developing because they reframe ideals and encourage public debate. At the least, they may spur gratuitous compassionate responses from authorities, which, although arbitrary, do save lives and preserve dignity. After Hurricane Katrina, President George Bush signed the bill requiring states to provide for pet safety in disasters[4]; during the wildfires in Southern California in October 2007, official action against illegal immigration was reported to be partly curtailed, and there appeared to be adequate emergency facilities for evacuees with proof of citizenship or legal residence who could not afford hotels[5]; President Bush directed the Federal Aviation Administration and exhorted the airlines to minimize delays during the 2007 holiday season, and the airlines pledged compliance.[6] Compared to what was not done during Hurricane Katrina, these are all only gestures, but they reveal an ongoing concern for the appearance of compassion and benevolence, which reinforces compassion and benevolence as public virtues.

Anthropologists and social critics distinguish between *shame cultures* and *guilt cultures*. Shame cultures have dominant groups with stringent codes of honor and decorum, and individual moral status depends on the opinion of high-status peers. Guilt cultures are less hierarchical, and their focus on individual responsibility and conscience allows for greater independence of moral status from the views of others. Homeric Greece is famously a shame culture, whereas the Christian-Judaic tradition has produced guilt cultures. To the extent that it views itself as a Christian, individualistic, classless society, the United States is a guilt culture. But to the extent that the media immediately publicizes what the rich, powerful, and famous, particularly politicians, do and say, we are a shame culture.

Ordinary white people who hold racists views and treat people of color aversively or disrespectfully are not usually punished, apart from the negative judgments of some of those who know them. But elected and appointed political figures, top executives of major corporations, and celebrities cannot make racist remarks or be perceived as racists without incurring very bad press or losing their jobs. It is now shameful for the elite to be known as racist. The intelligentsia usually keeps its collective moral eye on the behavior of the rich and powerful with the help of the media. And one way in which the media does guard democracy is by the use and threat of scandal.

However, this system of moral vigilance, which can achieve social justice by means of public shame, is inherently arbitrary. Shame cultures are only as moral as the standard to which the elite are held. American mores change from one decade to the next, and any sensational story may be eclipsed by a bigger one. The media and public do a poor job of distinguishing between the importance of private moral misdeeds and immoral actions that substantially affect human welfare. (Sexual misconduct can receive as much attention as economic or political betrayals of public trust.) Still, as the public's intolerance of racism displayed by the elite shows, some of the worst forms of contemporary public shame involve injuries to the dignity of others. However, while this preserves general standards of human dignity, the victims of insult, abuse, or neglect, which it was shameful for others to inflict on them, are inevitably shamed as well. This is because shame, unlike guilt, tarnishes victims as well as perpetrators.

SOCIAL INEQUALITY AND DISASTER

The pragmatics of shame are limited. Public figures and others of status can be shamed for specific deeds, but there is no mechanism to shame them for the long-term benefits that they derive from the misfortunes of others because they so often mistake their status for their personal character. What they own is fully theirs, according to their right to private property: If they have made their own fortune, they deserve it, regardless of who suffered in the process. If they have inherited what they own, then their status is even higher because their money is "older," no matter how their ancestors acquired wealth. Although the strategic uses of shame cannot be overlooked, when moral conscience is lax (i.e., when there are no promptings by conscience and no feelings of guilt after misbehavior), principled cultural criticism, based on enduring ideals, remains important. It would be more principled than using shame and guilt and probably lead to sounder changes in institutional structures if racism in disaster were effectively addressed, first, in moral cultural criticism, second, in legal argument, and third, in changes in laws and policies.

If the factor of nonwhite race is held constant in American society, there is great socioeconomic diversity within each racial group, and class does not neatly line up with race. For example, there are affluent blacks who live better than many whites. But if social class is held constant, then within each income group, blacks and other minorities fare worse than whites in education, employment status, criminal incarceration, and overall health. In the United States, the most disadvantaged groups are constituted by combinations of nonwhite race and poverty. The lack of disaster preparation by, and for, the most disadvantaged in itself further disadvantages them. (For instance, lost wages may result in homelessness for renters.) In other parts of the world, the most disadvantaged intersections may be the result of class and ethnicity, nationality, or religion, but the principle is the same: *disaster magnifies social inequality.*

Middle-class people who survive disasters without prior preparation can recover their predisaster lives and assets with time and effort. The rich fare even better. Naomi Klein notes that Help Jet, an airline in West Palm Beach, Florida, advertises "the first hurricane escape plan that turns a hurricane evacuation into a jet-setter vacation"

> Upon storm warnings, reservations are made for passengers at five-star golf resorts, spas, or Disneyland. Evacuees leave the hurricane zone on a thirty passenger turboprop: "No standing in lines, no hassle with crowds, just a first class experience that turns a problem into a vacation. . . . Enjoy the feeling of avoiding the usual hurricane evacuation nightmare."[7]

Passengers can bring their pets.[8] Membership is $500 a year, and round-trip airfare cost about $2,000 during the 2006 hurricane season. (Talk about "white flight"!)

The average disaster survivor is often imagined to be an able-bodied, young or middle-aged, white male. He is the likely hero, the norm for a traditional majority of the American population, and he is in fact the norm from the perspective of emergency workers and the military, even though both institutions are becoming increasingly diverse in race and gender. In civilian disasters, women, children, the elderly, the poor, recent immigrants, the disabled, and racial minorities have prior disadvantages compared to this norm, some self-evident in terms of physical capabilities and stamina, some subtler in terms of social bias. The ideal of egalitarian disaster assistance would be for those assisting to have enough supplies and personnel available to be speedily dispatched so as to dispense goods and services fairly in order to meet everyone's needs. Many think that this is exactly what did not happen after Hurricane Katrina. (Studies of what went wrong in New Orleans will probably ground the careers of a generation of academics and practitioners—unless/until there is a worse event.)

HURRICANE KATRINA

The undisputed facts two years after the event, were these. Hurricane Katrina was the most destructive natural disaster in American history, surpassing the Chicago fire of 1871, the San Francisco earthquake and fire of 1906, and Hurricane Andrew in 1992. Over $100 billion in damage resulted, extending 103 miles from Katrina's center, covering 93,000 square miles and 138 parishes and counties. Levees were overwhelmed on the lowest parts of the Mississippi River and Lake Pontchartrain. Three canals flooded in New Orleans, affecting 80 percent of the city. An estimated three hundred thousand homes were destroyed or left uninhabitable. There was additional destruction to commercial buildings, forests, and green spaces, with debris of 118 million cubic yards (over ten miles high if stacked on a football field).

After Katrina, the unemployment rate doubled from 6 to 12 percent in the hardest hit parts of Louisiana and Mississippi. One-fifth of the yearly output of oil production in the Gulf of Mexico was unused due to Hurricane Katrina and also Hurricane Rita, which struck on the border between Louisiana and Texas on September 24, 2005. There was spillage of 7.4 million gallons of oil into Gulf Coast waterways. In addition to environmental damage and pollution from standing water, sewage, chemicals, and human and animal remains, there was damage to 466 chemical facilities, 31 hazardous-waste sites, 16 Superfund toxic-waste sites, 170 drinking-water facilities, and dozens of wastewater treatment facilities.

Estimates of Katrina deaths over the region range from thirteen to fifteen hundred. About 80 percent of these deaths were in New Orleans. In Louisiana, 51 percent of those who died were older than sixty, and 47 percent were older than seventy-five. By February 2006, two hundred bodies remained unclaimed at the Victim Identification Center in Carville, Louisiana, and over two thousand people were still reported missing. Three quarters of a million people were displaced, many without vital documents, medical records, or insurance information. In August 2005, 1.1 million people over age sixteen evacuated, and approximately 267,000, 80 percent of whom were black, had not returned by the fall of 2007.[9]

Governor Kathleen Blanco of Louisiana declared a state of emergency on Friday, August 26, 2005. In response to her request, on August 27, President Bush declared a federal state of emergency for Louisiana and gave FEMA authority to mobilize whatever rescue efforts were needed. Also, on the evening of August 27, Governor Blanco made a personal plea to President Bush on behalf of storm victims in Louisiana for "everything you've got." On August 28, Katrina was upgraded to a category 5 storm, and the National Weather Service warned that power outages would last for weeks and "water shortages [would] make human suffering incredible by modern standards." Mayor Ray Nagin of New Orleans ordered an evacuation of the city. Michael Brown, Director of FEMA, and President Bush were briefed by Max Mayfield, Director of the National Hurricane Center, and told that the levees could be "topped." Katrina made landfall at 7 a.m. on Monday, August 29, as a category 4 hurricane. That morning, Mayor Nagin reported on *The Today Show* that water was coming over levees. Brown only asked Michael Chertoff, Secretary of FEMA, for one thousand Homeland Security employees to be dispatched to the Gulf Coast five hours after the storm hit. It then took FEMA personnel two days to get to New Orleans. President Bush flew over the region on Friday, September 2, the fifth day after the storm hit, and expressed sympathy for Mississippi senator Trent Lott, who lost his house.

Louisiana is the second poorest state in the United States. The residents of New Orleans were 63 percent black, half with incomes below the poverty line. Almost 60 percent of the poor black households in New Orleans lacked a vehicle, so many could not leave the city when the evacuation was ordered the day before the storm. After Katrina made land fall, it took five days for significant aid to arrive, and the only official assistance from city government was advice that those flooded out of their homes get to the Superdome to wait for buses out of the city.[10]

Multigenerational poverty in America makes people more vulnerable in disasters. All over the world, the poor are less physically mobile than those with more money. This is due to partly obvious economics (e.g., no cars in the Katrina case) and partly to the fact that the poor often have close familial and neighborhood ties in one specific place. New Orleans was not just any place but one of the richest cultural and historical cities in the United States. It could easily have been predicted that many of the poor in New Orleans would not be willing or able to follow a general order to evacuate and that relocation would represent deep cultural and personal hardships for them.[11]

After FEMA's initial assistance, which was extended several times, there was no government policy to support a return home for the poor who wanted to go back. On the contrary, there is evidence that the post-Katrina power structure in New Orleans immediately had a vision for development that would exclude the relocated black poor. Julian Bond notes that soon after the storm, in a meeting between Mayor Nagin and the Urban Land Institute, an organization of corporate land developers, there was a proposal of "forced mass buyouts of low-lying neighborhoods, including the Ninth

Ward, for conversion into 'green corridors.'" Bond also quotes a study of the Center for Social Inclusion:

> The unfortunate truth is, in evaluating the ability of New Orleans' residents to return . . . under current policies and fundings, few communities can be expected to recover. Most of those who have returned, or will be able to return or relocate to the New Orleans Metropolitan region, will be white and relatively well-off.[12]

Institutional Genocide?

One may wonder, as many have already, how it was possible for one hundred thousand Americans to be so abused and neglected at the same time. The large number might provide a clue. Americans pride themselves on egalitarianism in the treatment of individuals, and all of the nondiscrimination language in founding documents, constitutional amendments, and the civil rights and immigration-reform legislation of the 1960s refers to what may not be done to individuals. Historically, bigots and racists who have held the worst beliefs about minorities have often made exceptions for a few individuals. The worst beliefs, which is to say, the most malign and degrading myths and stereotypes, are reserved for the majorities of despised groups.

The images and rumors of crimes committed by black Katrina victims were an integral part of delayed rescue efforts. In "Disasters, Race and Disability," Lashmi Fjord notes that in the U.S. House of Representatives' Katrina Report, there was criticism of the administration's reliance for information on media reports rather than satellite images or communication with on-site experts.[13] Alongside the tragic pictures of stranded evacuees and people stuck on rooftops, there were pictures and reports of "looting" by blacks, which have been contrasted with depictions of whites doing the same thing, but with noncriminal descriptions (e.g., "finding food" versus "stealing"). The media also reported rumors of snipers firing on rescue helicopters, a seven-year-old rape victim whose throat had been slit, and thirty or forty dead bodies stacked in the Convention Center freezer. The U.S. House of Representatives' report laid to rest as false the rumors of the snipers, rape, and stacked dead bodies, but only after a year had passed. When the rumors were circulating, the National Guard entered the city with guns in position, ready to "pacify" the mass so that it could be rescued. Thus,

> The reports of rampant lawlessness, especially the persistent urban legend of shooting at helicopters definitely delayed some emergency and law enforcement responses. The National Guard refused to approach the Convention Center until September 2, 100 hours after the hurricane because "we waited until we

had enough force in place to do an overwhelming force," Lieutenant General H. Steven Blum, Chief of the National Guard Bureau told reporters on September 5, 2005 (*The Katrina Report 2005* [171]).[14]

But,

> One of my good friends, Col. Jacque Thibodeau, led that security effort. They said, "Jacques, you gotta get down here and sweep this thing." He says he was braced for anything. And he encountered nothing—other than a whole lot of people clapping and cheering and so glad they were there (Major Ed Bush, *The Katrina Report 2005*, [171]).[15]

From the perspective of FEMA, the president, and the viewing public, including African Americans (e.g., Secretary of State Condoleeza Rice, who was reportedly "out on the town" in New York City, buying shoes, dining, watching a Broadway show[16]), everything necessary was being done in those first hundred hours. On the Friday he visited New Orleans (the fifth day), George Bush said to Michael Brown, Director of FEMA, "Brownie, you're doing a heckuva job."[17]

Of course, we now know, and will continue to learn for many years, how the reality was different from the initial accounts based on stereotypes. The reality traumatized victims as it betrayed their trust. Can anyone who has experienced what Clarice Buter, a nurses' assistant for twenty-eight years, experienced on the interstate in New Orleans dismiss the following as a paranoid utterance?

> They tried to kill us. When you keep people on top of the interstate for five days, with no food and water, that's killing people. . . . Helicopters at night shining a light down on us. They know we was there. Policemen, the army, the whole nine yards, ambulance passing us up like we wasn't nothing. . . . We was treated worse than an animal.[18]

Stereotypes of a large group of people can fuel the plot of a "script" for what is believed likely to happen. When the group is stereotyped as incompetent and criminal, observers may expect the group to perish if it does not resort to crime.[19] If those observers are also a source of assistance, such a belief can become a self-fulfilling prophecy. People are less inclined to help those who are incompetent and criminal than they are the able and innocent. In that sense, *there is not safety but danger in numbers.* What happened in New Orleans after Hurricane Katrina was not exactly genocide or attempted genocide because the survival of the whole population of African Americans was not at stake, and there is no evidence of intention to kill the whole group or even all members residing in New Orleans. But one hundred thousand is a large number by anyone's standards, there was life-threatening neglect, and the victims were already socially despised in accord with current negative stereotypes of the "inner-city poor."

The concept of institutional racism has been a staple of critical race discourse since the 1960s.[20] African Americans and other nonwhites may experience exclusion and discriminatory harms in their dealings with institutions, organizations, and even individuals, without white individuals intending them harm on the grounds of race. Poverty and lack of education, which is more prevalent in nonwhite than white communities, may be the result of intergenerational disadvantage that persists without ongoing ill will, bad intentions, or overt racist action on the part of privileged individuals. It is now broadly understood that disadvantage associated with race can persist and even occur anew in the absence of racists. However, the Katrina episode, together with the history of institutionalized racism in the United States, suggests a more intense version of institutional racism in a very disturbing equation:

Prior disadvantage + disaster = *institutional genocide*

Indeed, the rage, frustration, and grief felt by Katrina's victims and many serious onlookers exceed a reaction to the statistics of the disaster itself. It suggests a fear and horror at the specter of a more general tragedy. The tragedy in this case goes beyond the vulnerability of the poor to disasters or the now indisputable facts of prior institutional racism. Of course, the poor, especially the black poor, are vulnerable. But in normal times, their exclusion from many of the goods of white middle-class life occurs over long periods. Institutionalized racism is a pervasive, but often subtle, social problem, a condition. However, when just one aspect of institutionalized racism, namely segregated housing, is combined with disaster in a context of ongoing racial aversion and dismissal of suffering, it becomes more likely for large numbers to perish at once. When a segregated community is beset with a disaster, there are no opportunities for individuals to avoid dehumanizing identities and neglectful treatment by those who perceive the whole group under negative stereotypes. There is no time or space for individuals to escape. The net result looks like a very horrible new thing: *institutionalized genocide*. Something very like Katrina could happen again, and it could be bigger.

In normal life, many of the poor are able to "pass" as not poor because they share the same mass culture with the rich and middle class. They watch the same television shows, eat the same food, aspire to the same luxury items, worship the same deities. As Jerry Springer has observed, the main difference between the people living on Park Avenue and in Beverly Hills and those who basked in the five minutes of fame he provided was money. It has been claimed that poverty is relative, meaning that the poor in America are economically better off than the poor in many other countries, particularly in the "third world." But the other side of that relativity is the gap in economic and social resources between rich and poor in a country that is, for the most part, rich. Where extreme American poverty is comparable to living conditions in some third world countries, it turns out to be "relatively" worse because of the size of that gap between our own rich and poor. This relegates the American poor to a kind of fourth world. Add black race and its associated stereotypes and lack of opportunity, and we have a "fifth world." Now add disaster to black American poverty, and the result is the aftermath of Hurricane Katrina, a "sixth world," its own circle of hell.

CONSPIRACY THEORY

Suppose that "institutional genocide" and "the sixth world" were *intended* by ruling elites and others in positions to benefit from eliminating specified groups of the poor. Suppose, also, that instead of white supremacy, or something like it, the guiding ideology was economic and the leading vice was not racism[21] but greed, greed of the sort that holds $10 billion dollars to be ten times as good as $1 billion. Greed like that, motivating not Marvel comic villains but real people who enjoy the support of government power, may already be a dominant factor in contemporary disaster as well as war. With this in mind, it is then a small step to imagine that the greedy villains welcome—if they do not directly cause—disaster as well as war. This brings us to the threshold of *conspiracy theory*. Conspiracy theorists generate the most cynical analyses of events like Hurricane Katrina and the most depressing prognoses for the future. Worth consideration in this regard is Naomi Klein's *The Shock Doctrine: The Rise of Disaster Capitalism* (2007).[22]

Klein claims to explain the global turn to a free market economy, which began during the last quarter of the twentieth century. Her thesis is that the growing power of international corporations and the decline of both socialism and paternalistic, or welfare, government were the result not of popular preference but great coercion. The coercers, according to Klein, were the University of Chicago economist Milton Friedman's protégés and their associates. Friedman taught his students, some of whom went on to influential careers in government, the absolute value of "free markets" to regulate human society. Although his ideas were not popular until after President Ronald Reagan assumed office, Friedman and his followers were willing to wait until the right opportunities to dismantle welfare states presented themselves.

According to Klein, Friedman's followers believed that when people are in a state of shock after an abrupt disruption of their normal lives, as after a military or terrorist attack or a natural disaster, they will offer less resistance to those neoconservative or *neoliberal* economic changes necessary to restore or create free markets. The term *shock*, in addition to referring to the psychic side of disruptive events, also literally refers to clinical uses of electroshock therapy for mental patients, covert CIA-backed research into extreme applications of such therapy, and torture. When people are sufficiently shocked in any of the relevant ways, their minds are open and blank, and they can be reeducated, or "reprogrammed." Klein claims that masses of shock victims have been coerced in exactly this way.

Here are some of Klein's international political examples: In the 1950s, Friedman advised the Chilean dictator Augusto Pinochet on implementing tax cuts, free trade, and reductions in social services, and he was also influential in Argentina's imposition of free market reforms accompanied by the "disappearance" of thirty thousand leftists. In 1982, British prime minister Margaret Thatcher, a close correspondent of Friedman's, turned her low approval ratings around after victory in the Falkland Islands. The excitement generated by patriotic celebration of the military victory allowed Thatcher to crush striking coal miners in the United Kingdom and instigate broad privatization of other utilities, as well as to encourage rampant corporate capitalism. In 1989, China's Communist government used the shock of the Tiananmen Square massacre to shift that country's entire economy to an export-base. In 1993, Boris Yeltsin, the first president of the Russian Federation, sent tanks to burn parliament buildings and lock up opposition leaders, creating a mass shock that cleared the way for his program of privatization and oligarchy.

When the Twin Towers were destroyed on 9/11, the White House contained many Friedman disciples, including his close friend Secretary of Defense Donald Rumsfeld. Klein claims that the goal of this cohort was to conduct the "Global War on Terror" by using private companies, which would lead to a privatization of government itself. Their program continued into the Iraq War, when between 2003 and 2006, the number of contracts for security functions increased from 3,512, to 115,000.[23]

As Klein interprets it, the project of privatization has extended into "disaster capitalism." In Sri Lanka, after the 2004 tsunami, the poor who lived along the coast and got their living from fishing were barred from returning home, and the government sold their land to luxury resort entrepreneurs. Klein reports that in the summer of 2004, FEMA rejected the state of Louisiana's request for funding of a contingency plan for a major hurricane. Instead, FEMA awarded a contract to a private firm, Innovative Emergency Management, to develop a hurricane disaster plan for southeastern Louisiana and New Orleans. At the cost of $1 million, detailed and sensible plans for evacuation, water delivery, and instant trailer parks were submitted, but FEMA never acted upon them due to a shortage of funds. Two weeks after Katrina hit, the Heritage Foundation hosted a meeting with

Republican lawmakers, and they developed thirty-two ideas for "hurricane relief," including suspension of prevailing wage laws and vouchers for charter schools. Companies employed in Iraq, such as Halliburton, Blackwater, Parsons, Fluor, Shaw, Bechtel, and CH2M Hill, all received lucrative contracts for reconstruction services in New Orleans.

In addition, there were apparently many "indirect costs" in the privatization of Katrina. Klein provides the following examples. Kenyon, a division of the funeral conglomerate Service Corporation International, had the contract to remove dead bodies at $12,500 each; although Kenyon worked slowly (with results visible to the entire world), local morticians and volunteers were barred from helping. Shaw charged FEMA $175 a square foot to install blue tarps provided by the government on damaged roofs, but the workers received $2 a square foot. (The overall reconstruction workforce was at least one-quarter Hispanic illegal immigrants.) Lighthouse Disaster Relief, the company paid $5.2 million by FEMA to construct a base camp for emergency workers in St. Bernard Parish, never completed this project and was in fact a religious group with prior experience only in building youth camps.[24] Klein suggests that these abuses are related to a type of corruption, whereby large corporations, after extensive lobbying and hefty campaign contributions, get contracts from the U.S. government, which they are not obligated to fulfill honestly. She writes,

> According to the *New York Times*, "the top service contractors have spent nearly $300 million since 2000 on lobbying and have donated $23 million to political campaigns." The Bush administration, in turn, increased the amount spent on contractors by roughly $200 billion between 2000 and 2006.[25]

The biggest problem with Klein's account of contemporary disaster is its *Manichaeanism*. The reader is invited to reason from seemingly independent incidents and structures to a malevolent whole, which in turn gives meaning to its components. The result is a totally bleak picture of contemporary life, without direct evidence that there is a hidden, conspiratorial group that is able to plan contemporary disasters for the sole overriding purpose of slaking its own greed. For instance, it is unlikely that all of 115,000 security-related government contracts were executed fraudulently. Some unprincipled and greedy agents do have great power, and they on occasion have opportunities to cooperate in ways that harm large numbers. But it is a huge leap beyond available evidence to hold such groups responsible for all recent disasters. They may indeed begin wars, but others have to carry them out through their own efforts—or refuse to do so. And they may profit from natural catastrophes, but there is no evidence that they can create those catastrophes or that they are the only interests represented in responses to them. Capitalism, consumerism, the depletion and destruction of natural resources, oppression, and the inheritance of social disadvantage are all part of contemporary reality, but so is cooperation, productivity, conservation, liberation, and opportunity.

The construction and entertainment of conspiracy theories exhausts civic energy in outrage so that autonomous agents are distracted from their own empowerment and plans for action. Utopias envisioned as an alternative to the source of outrage can induce a paralysis of the will to work for small change because those utopias are so clearly unattainable.[26] As Klein herself notes in the conclusion to *The Shock Doctrine*, there have already been political reversals of many of the policies she attributes to Friedman, in Latin American and Europe, once initial "shock" has worn off and people who have seen where their interests lie have begun to organize for change.[27] Such efforts and achievements could not have occurred if disaster capitalism and politics were always the monolithic system Klein implies.

DISASTER ACTIVISM

The poor, as a mass, are not the same as the poor as individuals or the poor in small groups or neighborhoods. I have argued that there is not necessarily "strength in numbers" in terms of what will be done to people or withheld from them. But obviously, two or six can accomplish more than one on the level of individuals. Perhaps we can assume that there is strength in numbers if we are talking about the addition of *persons* rather than mere numbers that amount to a stereotyped aggregate that is objectified by others. As people, "the poor" are not intrinsically helpless, and what happened in New Orleans need not be repeated, even if there is no change in government policy. Any small group can prepare for disaster by dividing labor, learning about evacuation routes, storing food, water, and extra clothing, and thinking about what they would do and what their normal obligations to care for themselves and others require them to do in disaster. Collecting rain water, basic first aid, and light search and rescue are examples of survival skills now within the reach of all U.S. residents. Every community in the United States now has some form of workplace, school, government, civic, volunteer, or do-it-yourself disaster-preparation resource. FEMA and the Red Cross have instructions and information, including lists of necessary supplies, online.

Everybody who has dependents, whether professionally or personally, can begin to figure out what their needs will be in a disaster. People need to assess their disaster-related skills, assets, and liabilities and think about what they will do in unwanted, but predicted, contingencies before they happen. Given what is already broadly known about the gaps in public and government disaster preparation and response, this is now a moral responsibility for individuals. Every disaster has had its compassionate and tireless volunteers. Ideally, all capable people would have some skill or resource qualifying them to help others—not solely for altruistic reasons but because those who are prepared to help others are less likely to become helpless victims themselves.

CAPITALISM AND DISASTER

The issue is not whether private industry or government best provides vital goods and services, including disaster relief, but whether those goods and services are the best possible given available resources and what power the end user or consumer has. What we don't *need*, in order to prepare for disaster (although some might like it, and the shift may or may not have merits on other grounds), is a fundamental change away from capitalism, or even global corporate capitalism. The major problem is not "privatization of government services," because the abuses Naomi Klein and others documented are not due to that alone.

If government services for the military and disaster relief had in reality been privatized according to core capitalistic principles and not merely baptized (by both supporters and critics) with the name, it could have happened in two ways: The government (either federal or state with federal financing) could have awarded contracts to the best companies according to public criteria for their capabilities. Or, it could have provided the end consuming units with vouchers to purchase what they needed from competing sources. Neither happened; instead, contracts in Iraq and New Orleans were awarded to private companies, sometimes in the absence of competitive bids, without public disclosure of criteria. In the absence of vouchers, end consumers, whether disaster victims or occupied Iraqis and relevant military purchasers, had no ability to choose among competing purveyors of goods and services.

Let's assume that the tax money making up the federal budget is constant at any given time. It makes no difference to that budget whether individual or institutional consuming and using units are given goods and services in kind or vouchers (from tax money) to buy them. Charter schools and vouchers for them, where the schools are run by competing private companies that pay the teachers' salaries, are examples of privatized education. But if only one company, paid by the government, furnishes education, funerary services, or roof repair, either freely or in exchange for vouchers,[28] that is not "privatization" or even "monopoly capitalism." Insofar as end consumers have no choice and there has been no competition for contracts, it is government-protected *monopoly*. This is ironic in light of Friedman-inspired aims to "privatize government." Instead of getting out of the picture, government has become more powerful by conferring its patronage without public disclosure of the merits of its chosen contractors (and subcontractors).

It is a contingent matter whether certain goods and services can best be provided, at any given time and place, by government employees or those paid by private firms. For example, in some societies, public education dispenses propaganda, public food is inadequate and not nutritious, and public health care does not meet basic medical needs. In other societies, all of these failures attend private sales of education, food, and health care. To call the recent no-bid/no-choice abuses of our *representational* system "privatization," "outsourcing," or "global corporate capitalism," and to assume those terms diagnose important problems, is to avoid the importance of standards for vital goods and services and to overlook the democratic value of consumer autonomy. In a democratic society, it should not be presumed that those governed are passive in the hands of kind or mean government. The real focus should be on the activity of those governed: the people.

SPIKE LEE'S VIEW OF THE DISADVANTAGED AFTER KATRINA

In principle, disaster is an equal opportunity event. A storm does not choose its victims. But, thus far, and not only in the United States, typical civilian disaster victims are already socially, economically, and politically disadvantaged. If this were always to be the case, for every foreseeable disaster, it would merit a completely socially constructivist approach to civilian disaster. "Civilian disaster" would mean "sudden misfortune in loss of life, well-being, and property that befalls a group or area of society that is already disadvantaged compared to other groups and areas." To an extent, this approach is assumed in some liberal representations of contemporary disaster, for example, in Spike Lee's *When the Levees Broke: A Requiem in Four Acts* (2006), which bears the additional subtitle "An American Tragedy."

Lee's documentary depicts the historical disadvantage of the African American victims of Hurricane Katrina. Shots of grieving over personal and material losses, references to the history of slavery, dramatic vignettes of interviewees' strong sense of place and home, and the jazz soundtracks throughout—all of these convey a distinctive Black culture with a rich background. Most of the displaced New Orleans residents were working people and homeowners, but once displaced, they had few or no material resources. Part of the recovery efforts in New Orleans resulted in the employment of Hispanic migrant workers to rebuild the city instead of unemployed black people. As Lee's subjects complain about this economic "slight" and those who are making money by seizing land and dwellings, a familiar historical theme, reminiscent of slavery and the general exploitation and dispersal of black people, is evoked. Lee sets this bleak tone early on with his replay of media footage of Konye West saying, "President Bush doesn't care about black people."

No whites in Lee's film appear as subjects expressing racist views. Several of Lee's subjects bitterly denounced Barbara Bush's comment that the Katrina refugees in the Houston Astrodome benefited from the storm, but she herself is not presented directly. Thus, Lee's documentary represents the effects of white institutional racism, as his interviewees cope with a de facto racist catastrophe that has unfolded in the absence of racists. Again, well before Katrina, African Americans had already been excluded and discriminated against on economic or cultural grounds without race, per se, ever being an explicit issue.[29]

Still, the disaster depicted is not wholly free of classic, intentional racism. A black interviewee describes being shot by whites using racist language against him and his cousin. Experiences of racism as direct hatred are expressed by black New Orleans residents who report having heard explosions when Katrina hit. Several of Lee's interviewees believe that the levees were bombed to spare white neighborhoods at the expense of black ones, something known to have occurred during the Great Flood of 1927. One 2005 New Orleans hurricane victim, who relocated to New York City, says she would not return home so that they could "finish me off." Black survivors recalling the first days after the storm recount incidents of helicopters passing them overhead, despite their desperate pleas and signs for help.

Unfolding from the storm warnings, to footage of storm destruction, to rescue and response efforts, to attempts at reconstruction and recovery, the four acts of *When the Levees Broke* tell a big story of American civilization from an African American perspective. In evoking the historical as well as contemporary disaster-based effects of racism, *When the Levees Broke* develops as a seemingly natural indictment of the Army Corp of Engineers, corrupt state and city government, and President George W. Bush. It is repeatedly made clear that the response to the hurricane and the delay and negligence in recovery efforts constituted the disaster, which was merely precipitated by the storm. A local journalist claims that it was not the hurricane that caused the devastation but poorly engineered levees that could not withstand even a category 1 or 2 surge from Lake Pontchartrain.

A WIDER VIEW

Both "shock doctrine" types of conspiracy or near-conspiracy theories and the near-paranoia expressed by Spike Lee's subjects yield valuable insights, while they fall short of literal truths. Klein neither suggests nor establishes a full-blown behind-the-scenes conspiracy.[30] Her account proceeds "as if" government leaders have systematically attempted to implement a program for developing free markets, which was first proposed by Milton Friedman. Similarly, Lee's subjects do not engage in well-developed "theories" about the causes of their plight; their assessments of their situation proceed "as if" top government leaders "did not like black people." The valuable insights in both cases point to failures in both the transparency and effectiveness of government entities, which we must assume in a democratic society with egalitarian ideals can be improved.

Moreover, on the issue of race and racism, we should note that racism against poor African Americans is not the whole story about what went wrong, or what was right, in the response to Katrina. Spike Lee made no attempt at a thorough description of the storm dynamics of Hurricane Katrina, the problems with the models of hurricanes used by engineers, or the complexity of the weather conditions in New Orleans when Katrina hit.[31] Some disaster officials now believe that the response effort in New Orleans was successful in two ways: the U.S. Coast Guard rescued over thirty-three thousand[32]; the Houston Astrodome, dubbed "Reliant City," provided temporary shelter and living supplies for sixty-five thousand evacuees for twenty-one days, until it had to be evacuated because of Hurricane Rita.[33]

African Americans were not the only victims of Katrina.[34] In addition to the 850 African Americans, 550 whites died, and for 444 people, no race was specified. Although two white sisters, one emboldened by drinking beer, make stinging critical comments against government, little is said or shown in the documentary about the vulnerability of the elderly as a distinct group or the plight of the handicapped. For instance, Benilda Caixetta, a wheelchair-bound, middle-class, Hispanic woman, slowly drowned to death in her apartment after repeated assurances from contacts all over the country that she would be rescued.[35]

The conclusion to be drawn here is twofold. First, compassion for neglected and abused disaster victims and outrage at such injustice is well justified. But second, even in Katrina, prior disadvantage included at least disability and age, as well as race and class. Reasoning more broadly from Katrina, we can say that disaster preparation and response should be needs-based. This is because not all socially disadvantaged groups will necessarily suffer equal disadvantages in disasters, and any identity-based special preparations will likely be at least as contentious as Affirmative Action in normal times. Needs, be they for food, water, shelter, transportation for evacuation, or personal mobility assistance, translate directly into preparation and resource deployment in egalitarian ways. For a more trivial example, in the present mood of air travel, if many passengers would object if they heard that special arrangements were in place for handicapped travelers, which were being financed by increases in the price of all tickets. And more would protest if fare increases included funds for hiring additional personnel who could translate for non-English speaking passengers. But if a certain number of wheel chairs were said to be *needed*, and more service personnel were said to be *needed*, the reaction would probably be more generous.

NOTES

1. Patrick Creed and Rick Newman, *Firefight: Inside the Battle to Save the Pentagon on 9/11* (New York: Ballantine Books, 2008), 330.

2. Copyright 1964, renewed in 1992 by Special Rider Music.

3. For an account of the rest of Zantzinger's life and how Hattie Carolle's relatives remember her, see Ian Frazier, "Legacy of a Lonesome Death," *Mother Jones*, November/December 2004, at www.motherjones.com/commentary/slant/2004/11/10_200.html.

4. See press_releases/president_bush_signs_pets_Act.html.

5. One-third (two hundred of six hundred) of the border-patrol personnel were reassigned to help against the fires (see www.msnbc.msn.com/id/21437752). However, there were both news stories and television reports of illegal aliens kept working in smoke-filled conditions in tomato fields; a Mexican family of twelve, accused of looting in San Diego's Qualcomm Stadium, was summarily deported to Tijuana; many poor communities, including Native American reservations, were not evacuated, and their inhabitants were neglected by official sources of aid, including the Red Cross. Documented by Justin Akers Cacón, professor of Chicano Studies at the University of California, San Diego, in "Divided by Fire: Two San Diegos Emerge from the Flames," November 2, 2007, www.socialistworker.org/2007-2/651/651_06_Divided.shtml and www.dissidentvoice.org/author/JustinAkers.

6. See news.yahoo.com/s/ap/20071115/ap_on_go_pr_wh/airline_delays.

7. See www.helpjet.us.

8. Naomi Klein, *The Shock Doctrine: The Rise of Disaster Capitalism* (New York: Metropolitan Books, 2007), 415–16. Help jet's website is www.helpjet.us.

9. This account relies on the White House, "The Federal Response to Hurricane Katrina: Lessons Learned 5–9 (2006)," reprinted in Daniel A. Farber and Jim Chen, *Disasters and the Law: Katrina and Beyond* (New York: Aspen Publishers, 2006), 2–5. The report was written in February 2006, and at that time, the number of evacuees who had not returned was estimated at five hundred thousand. Writers in 2007 put it at about three hundred thousand. See, e.g., Julian Bond, "In Katrina's Wake," *Journal of Race and Policy* 3, Special Issue, *In Katrina's Wake: Racial Implications of the New Orleans Disaster* (spring/summer 2007): 27.

10. For this part of my account, I have mainly relied on Julian Bond, "In Katrina's Wake," 15–22, and Donald A. Saucier, Sara J. Smith, and Jessica L. McManus, "The Possible Role of Discrimination in the Rescue Response after Hurricane Katrina," *Journal of Race and Policy*, 113–14.

11. Martell L. Teasley, "Organizational Cultural Competence and Disaster Relief Participation," *Journal of Race and Policy*, 102–12.

12. Bond, "In Katrina's Wake," 28–29, from M. Davis, "Who Is Killing New Orleans?" *The Nation*, April 10, 2006, and the Center for Social Inclusion, "The Race to Rebuild: The Color of Opportunity and the Future of New Orleans," August 2006, www.centerforsocialinclusion.org/PDF/racetorebuild.pdf.

13. Lashmi Ford, "Disasters, Race and Disability: [Un]Seen Through the Political Lens on Katrina," *Journal of Race and Policy*, 46–65; House report cited on 46–47 as U.S. House of Representatives, *A Failure of Initiative: Final Report of the Select Bipartisan Committee to Investigate the Preparation for and Response to Hurricane Katrina*, 109th Congress, 2nd Session, H. Report 108-377. www.gpoaccess.gov/serialset/creports/katrina.html, February 15, 2006, 223.

14. Ford, "Disasters, Race and Disability," 52.

15. Ford, "Disasters, Race and Disability," 52.

16. Bond, "In Katrina's Wake," 18.

17. Bond, "In Katrina's Wake," 19, quoted from the White House, Office of the Press Secretary, 2005.

18. Bond, "In Katrina's Wake," 15, quoted from B. Ransby, "Katrina, Black Women, and the Deadly Discourse on Black Poverty in America," *DuBois Review* 3, no. 1 (spring 2006): 217.

19. Cf. Ford, "Disasters, Race and Disability," 46–65.

20. See Naomi Zack, "Race and Racial Discrimination," in *Oxford Handbook of Practical Ethics*, ed. Hugh Lafollette (Oxford: Oxford University Press), 2002, 2006, 245–71.

21. For discussion of how racism is a vice, see Zack, "Race and Racial Discrimination," 245–71.

22. Naomi Klein, *The Shock Doctrine: The Rise of Disaster Capitalism* (New York: Henry Holt, 2007).

23. Klein, *The Shock Doctrine*, 3–12.

24. Klein, *The Shock Doctrine*, 409–12. Many of Klein's sources are articles in the *New York Times*, which is to say that the arrangements she reports have hardly been a secret.

25. Klein, *The Shock Doctrine*, 412.

26. Indeed, the "consumption," as well as construction, of conspiracy theories that have flourished since 9/11 seems to be a substitute for realistic political engagement in some cases. See Mark Fenster, *Conspiracy Theories: Secrecy and Power in American Culture* (Minneapolis: University of Minnesota Press, 2008), esp. 279–91.

27. Klein, *The Shock Doctrine*, 424–66.

28. See Klein, *The Shock Doctrine*, 410–12.

29. See Naomi Zack, *Thinking about Race* (Belmont, CA: Thomson Wadsworth, 2006), ch. 5; Glenn C. Loury, *The Anatomy of Racial Inequality* (Cambridge, MA: Harvard University Press, 2002).

30. Such accounts, complete with secret powerful groups who form the real government in controlling mass events, are not wanting at this time. For instance, there is the post-9/11 Truth Movement, as documented by Fenster in *Conspiracy Theories*, 197–278. And, of course, there are the theories themselves, for example, the internet video *Zeitgeist: Addendum* and Daniel Estulin's *The Bilderberg Group* (Walterville, OR: Trineday, 2007).

31. See John Schwartz, "An Autopsy of Katrina: Four Storms, Not Just One," *New York Times*, May 30, 2008, available at www.nytimes.com/2006/05/30/science/30storm.html.

32. See "Coast Guard: Observations on the Preparation, Response, and Recovery Missions Related to Hurricane Katrina," GAO-06–903, U.S. Government Accountability Office, July 31, 2006, www.gao.gov/docsearch/abstract.php?rptno=GAO-06-903.

33. At the May 13–17, 2006, National CERT conference in Los Angeles, government officials presented films of the response to Hurricane Katrina that depicted their own success and heroism. CERT, or Citizens Emergency Response Team, is a national organization that offers standardized first-response training to volunteers in local communities.

34. The statistics on the deceased show substantial deaths in racial categories other than black, according to the list, below, maintained by Columbia University at www.katrinalist.columbia.edu/stats.php:

Breakdown of Race	
African American	830
Caucasian	553
Hispanic	36
Native American	6
Asian/Pacific Islander	14
Other	0
No race specified	444

35. June Isaacson Kailes, "Serving and Protecting All by Applying Lessons Learned—Improving Access to Disaster Services for People with Disabilities and Seniors," Center for Disability Issues and the Health Professions, 2005, www.jik.com/11-28-05%20CHHS_Draft_Report%20V1-3aRestricted.doc. See also www.benildacaixeta.com. The names and demographics of all 1,890 victims can be found at www.katrinalist.columbia.edu.

Conclusion

A Code of Ethics for Disaster, Its Implications, and the Water Crisis

The preceding chapters do not admit of a conclusion in the sense that anything has been "proved." Instead, to the extent that discussions have been persuasive, new subjects for further discussion become necessary as well as possible. I will therefore end this book with a code of ethics for disaster, a brief discussion of the implications of ethics for disaster, a suggestion that some long-standing social problems such as water shortage be viewed as disasters, and a code of ethics for the global water crisis.

A CODE OF ETHICS FOR DISASTER

A code of ethics for disaster is necessary because ethics generally involve human life and well-being, and disaster threatens these values. But before considering a code of ethics for disaster, several problems encountered during discussion in this book should be kept in mind:

1. The unpredictable nature of any disaster and its concrete details preclude developing specific lists of dos and don'ts that will apply to all disasters.
2. The conflicts between moral systems of consequentialism and deontology may result in incompatible general principles of action. While consequentialism seems practical, deontology is closer to our broadly held moral views—for instance, that we may not harm one another. And yet, disasters may necessitate unpredictable exceptions to such principles, calling for case-by-case analyses. The addition of virtue

125

ethics may fill in gaps left by both consequentialism and extensions of deontology, but we need to think critically about our preferred virtues.

3. The preparation and response obligations of private parties and government have not yet been widely discussed or accepted.

4. Existing popular views and government structures have combined issues of security and safety in ways that may be detrimental to public safety.

5. Disaster may damage human dignity in ways not addressed by legal policies for response.

6. Disaster has worse effects on those who are disadvantaged in normal times, but the biases that perpetuate social injustice are unlikely to change quickly during disaster preparation and response.

These problems have yielded tentative solutions in the course of analysis and discussion in the chapters of this book, and the following could serve to support further moral discussion.

Code of Ethics for Disaster

1. *General moral obligations:* There is a moral obligation to plan for, as well as respond to, disaster. Planning for disaster is part of both preparation and response, and disaster preparation and response are subject to moral evaluation. Disaster preparation and response should be based on assumptions of peaceful cooperation.

2. *Adequacy and fairness:* The moral system applied to disaster planning and response ought not to violate broad consensual intuitions about what human beings are permitted to do to one another in normal times. Moral decisions for probable or instant disasters require broad public discussion. Practices that are not egalitarian, due to limited resources, must be fair. The best principle of disaster planning is Fairly Save All Who Can Be Saved with the Best Preparation (FSALLBP).

3. *Individual responsibility:* Individuals are morally obligated to prepare for, and respond to, disaster in ways that will optimally preserve their own lives and well-being and those of their dependents. This obligation extends to helping neighbors, colleagues, and strangers, when there is no harm to the individuals or their dependents.

4. *Social contract obligations:* Democratic government was founded to make life better for those governed. Government is therefore obligated to assist individuals in disaster-preparation and -response planning and implementation, before its services are temporarily disrupted by disaster. Government is also required to plan and implement its own disaster preparation and response.

5. *Safety and security:* Issues of public safety should be treated distinctly from issues of public security, with jurisdictional cooperation among government entities.
6. *Dignity:* The human dignity of all disaster victims should be preserved as a primary moral value.
7. *Needs:* In disaster preparation and response, both private and government planners must address the needs of all victims.

IMPLICATIONS OF ETHICS FOR DISASTER

Definitions of disaster acquire a new importance after the moral dimension of disaster is considered. Human beings have always altered their environments to satisfy their needs and wants. Advances in technical expertise, scientific understanding, and moral concern for all human life and well-being have enabled more active, proactive, and critical attitudes to both natural and human-caused catastrophes. Now, accompanying definitions of disaster is the assumption that action can be taken to prevent, prepare for, and better respond to it. Our motivation and ability to interact with the causes and effects of disasters in this way enables the moral dimension of disaster. Not only does the claim that we ought to do something imply that we can do it, but what we can do invokes moral reflection because it affects our own and others' well-being.

Insofar as disasters are mass events that we do not want, the disaster-specific factor of human intervention and reaction can be extended to other mass events that we do not want, which are less compressed in time than events now considered disasters. Vehicular accidents, AIDs, world hunger, the civilian effects of war, and extreme financial crises are examples of extended events that could be considered disasters. Global warming is already recognized to be a cause of disasters. It should be noted that in affluent societies, some of these *risks*, such as vehicular accidents and financial crises are already treated as disasters in terms of response.

The inclusion of *all* destructive events or episodes with high human casualties that occur over longer periods of time than those we now consider disasters is more than a semantic matter. Once an event is categorized as a disaster, both private and public sectors become more directly mobilized and motivated to prevent, mitigate, prepare for, respond to, and recover from it. However, after very destructive events or conditions, such as AIDs, or global starvation, persist for a while, in the absence of the intense response associated with recognized disasters, people become habituated to them as "social problems" in normal life. Such habituation to catastrophe insulates those who are safe and could otherwise intervene, leading to the neglect of sufferers and victims. There may be objective improvement over time as the problems run their historical course or concerned individuals and small groups make humanitarian efforts to solve them, but the longer the process of habituation or normalization, the less the likelihood of compressed effective solutions.

The distinction between problematic normality and disaster is upheld as though an invisible clock were connected to the human "fight-or-flight" reaction to danger and stress. An intense fight-or-flight response apparently cannot be maintained, either individually or collectively, for more than short periods of time. When it is, pathology is diagnosed, for example, posttraumatic stress disorder (PTSD) if the crisis is in the past or "burn out" if an ongoing crisis is believed to have exceeded normal human abilities to cope effectively. Acceptable stress, as experienced by individuals and located in external events, has time limits determined by human psychology and physiology, as well as social and cultural factors. These ways of organizing individual experience reinforce the immense importance of what human beings consider to be "normal." In metaphorical and real similarity with other predatory species, our default mode of being in the world is calm, complacent, and lazy.

If disaster can be understood, organized, and moralized, which is to say, "tamed," then disaster itself becomes normalized. But we have to be careful here because it is so easy for those who are safe and privileged to tame for themselves what remains untamed for others. If what we already accept as normal for ourselves is "disasterized," new cycles of fight-or-flight responses, trauma, posttrauma, or ongoing stress may be activated. We should therefore be sure that we are able to mitigate, organize, rationalize, and moralize the new candidates for disaster. Otherwise, we will have upset ourselves with worry, fear, and futile combat for nothing or else depleted psychic and physical reserves that could be used more effectively in other crises. Our task is to recognize and tame disasters in the right way, without either slipping into denial about their dangers or exaggerating them. Some past opportunities to do this may have lapsed, but there is no shortage of future crises and disasters to which best efforts can and should be applied. Consider now the global water crisis.

THE GLOBAL WATER CRISIS

Every day in 2007, approximately sixteen thousand children died of starvation, or one every five seconds.[1] However, world hunger is now a well-established social problem rather than a disaster. If tomorrow sixteen thousand children were to die in Europe or the United States from particulates caused by fires or hurricanes, would that be a disaster? If sixteen thousand people died from a terrorist attack on American soil in one day, would that be a disaster?

World hunger has been going on for a long time, which works against its being considered a disaster, even though the facts of world hunger do merit that label. It is highly unlikely that world hunger will suddenly be considered a disaster. But what about the next big terrible thing with even more devastating consequences than world hunger? Will the shortage of water on earth be considered a disaster or a social problem, which is to say, an unfortunate condition of life for those who are already disadvantaged?

On March 15, 2009, the third edition of the *United Nations World Water Development Report* (WWDR-3) will be presented at the Fifth World Water forum in Istanbul, Turkey. WWDR-3 will have a holistic format incorporating new information on climate change, the UN Millennium Development Goals, ground water, biodiversity, infrastructure, biofuels, and related subjects, all under the supervision of relevant experts.[2] The facts about the world water shortage are not in dispute. At present, 1.2 billion people do not have access to safe water: almost 50 percent of the population of sub-Saharan Africa, 28 percent in Asia, 18 percent in Latin America, 88 percent in rural Ethiopia (forty million), half a billion in India. Of illness in developing nations, 80 percent is due to water pathogens, and half of all hospital beds are occupied by patients with water-related diseases. It is projected that by 2025, one-third of the world's population will lack safe drinking water and adequate sanitation.

The causes of the world water crisis are economic growth and population increase, global warming, lack of sanitation, and industrial and chemical pollution. Glaciers are melting, rivers are increasingly damned or diverted, aquifers are subject to depletion at increasing rates, and remaining sources of safe water are rapidly being appropriated by private commercial interests. Rising sea levels force salt water into fresh-water sources, and desalination projects are expensive and technologically demanding. Political conflicts over water could lead to war if they are not solved cooperatively. There is, moreover, a disproportionate use of water by the inhabitants of rich nations.[3]

One of the main differences between disasters and social problems is that a moral code for disaster has urgency due to the perceived time compression of disastrous events, whereas actions taken to solve social problems seem optional or deferrable because the social problems develop and persist over longer periods. But suppose that the world water shortage were considered a disaster. What would the Code of Ethics for Disaster imply for it?

Code of Ethics for the World Water Crisis

1. *General moral obligation:* There is a moral obligation to plan for increasing water shortage with mitigation projects. Whether those projects are well designed given present information, then well implemented, will

be subject to moral evaluation. Planning also requires that some forms of water usage be restricted and curtailed and that government entities and utilities create emergency supplies of fresh water for people in emerging shortage areas. Insofar as water sources are often in jurisdictions different from those in which water is consumed, to avoid conflict, cooperation is required in mitigating predicted water shortages and storing emergency water supplies. Moreover, the 1.2 billion people who currently suffer from the lack of safe water deserve immediate assistance on humanitarian grounds.

2. *Adequacy and fairness:* Applying FSALL is to the water shortage, at this time, creates an expectation that everyone who will suffer from water shortage can be saved. Fairness in emergency distribution of inadequate supplies of water ought not to disadvantage those societies and locations that lack water despite their prior best efforts at mitigation and emergency storage, and it might require sacrifice from those who are using more water than they need. That is, it may be that the fair allocation of scarce water resources will require a suspension of some existing property rights in water.

3. *Individual responsibility:* Individuals have a responsibility to secure enough water for themselves and their dependents to see them through both emergencies and long-term water shortages—to the extent that they are able.

4. *Social contract obligations:* Governments legitimized by their obligation to make life better for those under their jurisdiction are required to assist individuals in fulfilling their water responsibilities. Such legitimate democratic governments are also responsible for maintaining those sources of water for which government actions are required and acquiring new sources when those run out.

5. *Safety and security:* Safe and sufficient water is primarily a matter of public safety. Criminal and terrorist activities endangering safe and sufficient water ought to be addressed as distinct security issues.

6. *Dignity:* Human beings who do not have sufficient safe water should not on that account be devalued or treated with less respect than those who do, and their access to enough safe water should be viewed as a requirement for their dignity. Procuring and distributing water to those in need is a humanitarian ideal or moral obligation for those able to do so.

7. *Needs:* The amount of water needed to sustain physical life and maintain hygiene, as well as the water needed to support other human necessities, is less than the per capita amount consumed in rich, developed countries. The question of needs becomes difficult to address over the long term because it involves social-justice issues. However, human needs for water in emergency conditions where there is no wa-

ter are straightforward. The universal nature of human needs for water easily translates into a universal right. Former UN Secretary General Kofi Annan stated, "Access to safe water is a fundamental human need and, therefore, a basic human right. Contaminated water jeopardizes both the physical and social health of all people. It is an affront to human dignity."[4]

POSTSCRIPT: MORAL VERSUS MONETARY VALUES OF HUMAN LIFE

Throughout this book, it has been assumed that moral values—the primary one being human life—are absolute. To think morally is to reflect on matters that exceed economic choices and material goods. This may be naïve because, for example, there is a point at which money and other resources become relevant in saving or prolonging human life. Economists, insurance companies, and public-policy planners are sensitive to this last practical reality.

On July 11, 2008, the U.S. Environmental Protection Agency (EPA) received media attention for its monetary revaluation of an American human life. In May, the EPA had revised its figure from $7.8 to $6.9 million. This "value of statistical life" entails that the life-saving results of some practices can be balanced against their costs. A lower value of statistical life permits spending less money on life-saving practices. Statistical life is not measured according to earning capacity, value to society, or love and familial relationships; instead, it is based on what individuals would pay to avoid specific risks and how much extra they are paid for taking them on. The data for computing statistical life is compiled from payroll figures and surveys of public opinion. Thus, statistical life is not supposed to be a "price on life."[5] In many cases, U.S. statistical life is lower in value than jury awards in wrongful-death suits, although it is probably higher than the face value of most life-insurance policies. And it would also be higher than the statistical life values of those who live in countries without environmental protection administrations.

There was immediate public response to the EPA's lowering of the value of American statistical life by $900,000. Senator Barbara Boxer (D-CA) immediately called the reduction in value "outrageous" and pledged that she would introduce legislation to "reverse this unconscionable decision." Boxer ignored the economic foundation of statistical life, as based on documented economic decisions, and instead conflated it with an absolute value of human life. She said, "EPA may not think Americans are worth all that much, but the rest of us believe the value of an American life to our families, our communities, our workplaces and our nation is no less than it has ever been. This new math has got to go." It is noteworthy that Boxer's statement assumes that an appropriate monetary value could be placed on such otherwise nonmaterial values of human life and that the problem with the EPA's current figure for statistical life, as she misunderstood it, is that the figure is too low.

If monetary value can be placed on the worth of an individual's life to others, then presumably people who were less useful or had diminished capabilities would be worth less. In 2003, a U.S.-Canadian study measured willingness to pay for mortality reductions against respondents' age and health. It was found that respondents over age forty with heart or lung disease or cancer would willingly pay *more* to reduce their risk of dying than healthier and even younger people.[6]

The definition of statistical life is connected to the assumption that life can be priced in the dimensions of capabilities and value to others. The connection is that measures of statistical life depend on what people either willingly pay to avoid risk or demand in payment to assume risk. When people make these decisions, they are in effect performing economic self-valuations, or putting prices on their own lives. Much in U.S. culture, and indeed world resource differentials, supports the ability and reasonableness of putting prices on one's own life in this way. But moral reflection begins exactly at the point where this approach evokes disappointment, sadness, and principled objection on behalf of what it overlooks. Moral reflection on human life entails the impossibility of assigning it a monetary value. This means either that human life is worth nothing or that it is worth everything.

NOTES

1. Robert Black, Saul Morris, and Jennifer Bryce, "Where and Why Are 10 Million Children Dying Every Year?" *Lancet* 361 (2003): 2226–34.

2. See http://www.unesco.org/water/wwap/wwdr/wwdr3/ Millennium Development Goal #7 is: By 2015 reduce by half the proportion of people without sustainable access to safe water and sanitation.

3. On the disruption of the world's river systems, see Fred Pearce, *When the Rivers Run Dry: Water—The Defining Crisis of the Twenty-first Century* (Boston: Beacon Press, 2006). On the recent privatization of water-source appropriation and grassroots movements against the trend, see Maude Barlow, *Blue Covenant: The Global Water Crisis and the Coming Battle for the Right to Water* (New York: New Press, 2008).

4. Quoted in "Why WASRAG?" Water and Sanitation Rotarian Action Group, March 2008, www.wasrag.org/downloads/brochures/Join%20WASRAG%20Form.pdf.

5. See www.msnbc.msn.com/id/25626294.

6. Anna Albertini, Maureen Cropper, Alan Krupnick, and Nathalie B. Simon, "Does the Value of a Statistical Life Vary with Age and Health Status?" *Journal of Environmental Economics and Management* 48, no. 1 (July 2004): 769–92.

Select Bibliography

BOOKS AND ARTICLES

9/11 Commission Report: Final Report on the National Commission on Terrorist Attacks upon the United States. 1st ed. New York: W. W. Norton, n.d., 339–40.

A Failure of Initiative: Final Report of the Select Bipartisan Committee to Investigate the Preparation for and Response to Hurricane Katrina. 109th Congress, 2nd Session, February 15, 2006.

Albertini, Anna, Maureen Cropper, Alan Krupnick, and Nathalie B. Simon. "Does the Value of a Statistical Life Vary with Age and Health Status?" *Journal of Environmental Economics and Management* 48, no. 1 (July 2004): 769–92.

Aquinas, St. Thomas. *On Kingship.* Translated by G. B. Phelan and I. Th. Eschmann. Toronto: Pontifical Institute of Medieval Studies, 1959.

Aristotle. "Nichomachean Ethics." In *Basic Works of Aristotle,* edited by Richard McKeon. New York: Random House, 1941.

———. "Politics." In *Basic Works of Aristotle,* edited by Richard McKeon. New York: Random House, 1941.

Augustine, Saint. *The City of God.* Edited by R. W. Dyson. Cambridge, MA: Cambridge University Press, 1998.

Barlow, Maude. *Blue Covenant: The Global Water Crisis and the Coming Battle for the Right to Water.* New York: New Press, 2008.

Beck, Ulrich. *Risk Society: Toward a New Modernity.* London: Sage, 1992.

———. "Risk Society Revisited: Theory, Practice, and Research Programs." In *The Risk Society and Beyond: Critical Issues for Social Theory,* edited by Barbara Adam, Ulrich Beck, and Joost Van Loon, 211–29. London: Sage, 2000.

Bennett, Jonathan. "The Conscience of Huckleberry Finn." *Philosophy* 49 (1974): 123–34.

Bellavita, Christopher. "A Changing Homeland Security: The Issue-Attention Cycle." *Homeland Security Affairs* 1, no. 1 (summer 2005), www.hsaj.org/?article=1.1.1.

Bond, Julian. "In Katrina's Wake." *Journal of Race and Policy* 3, Special Issue, *In Katrina's Wake: Racial Implications of the New Orleans Disaster* (spring/summer 2007): 16–32.

Cacón, Justin Akers. "Divided by Fire: Two San Diegos Emerge from the Flames." October 30, 2007. www.socialistworker.org/2007–2/651/651_06_ and www .dissidentvoice.org/author/JustinAkers.

Community Emergency Response Team Participation Manual. Developed for Department of Homeland Security, United States Fire Administration, Emergency Management Institute, by Human Technology, Inc. McLean, Virginia, June 2003.

Creed, Patrick, and Rick Newman. *Firefight: Inside the Battle to Save the Pentagon on 9/11.* New York: Ballantine Books, 2008.

Didion, Joan. *Fixed Ideas.* New York: New York Review of Books, 2003.

Downs, Anthony. "The Issue-Attention Cycle." *Public Interest* 28 (summer 1972): 38–50.

Dynes, Russell R. "The Dialogue between Voltaire and Rousseau on the Lisbon Earthquake: The Emergence of a Social Science View." Disaster Research Center. www.udel.edu/DRC/preliminary/pp294.pdf.

Farber, Daniel A., and Jim Chen. *Disasters and the Law: Katrina and Beyond.* New York: Aspen Publishers, 2006.

Fenster, Mark. *Conspiracy Theories: Secrecy and Power in American Culture.* Minneapolis: University of Minnesota Press, 2008.

Flynn, Vince. *Act of Treason.* New York: Pocket Star Books, 2006.

———. *Consent to Kill.* New York: Pocket Star Books, 2003.

Ford, Lashmi. "Disasters, Race and Disability: [Un]Seen through the Political Lens on Katrina." *Journal of Race and Policy* 3, Special Issue, *In Katrina's Wake: Racial Implications of the New Orleans Disaster* (spring/summer 2007): 46–65.

Fuller, Lon L. "The Case of the Speluncean Explorers." *Harvard Law Review* 62, no. 4 (February 1949), www.nullapoena.de/stud/explorers.html.

Gibbs, W. Waut, and Christine Soares. "Preparing for a Pandemic: Are We Ready?" *Scientific American,* Special Report, November 2005.

Glendon, Mary Ann. *A World Made New: Eleanor Roosevelt and the Universal Declaration of Human Rights.* New York: Random House, 2001.

Gordon, Vikki. "The Law: Unilaterally Shaping U.S. National Security Policy: The Role of National Security Directives." *Presidential Studies Quarterly* 37, no. 2 (June 2007): 349–67.

Gostin, L. "Medical Countermeasures for Pandemic Influenza: Ethics and the Law." *Journal of the American Medical Association* 295 (2006): 554–56.

Haddow, George D., and Jane A. Bullock. *Introduction to Emergency Management.* Burlington, MA: Elsevier Science, 2003.

Harrington, Edward Michael. *The Other America: Poverty in the United States.* Baltimore, MD: Penguin Books, 1963.

Hegel, Wolfgang. *Philosophy of Right and Law,* translated by J. M. Sterrett and Carl J. Friedrich. In *The Philosophy of Hegel,* edited by Carl J. Friedrich. New York: Random House, 1953.

Hick, John L., and D. O'Laughlin. "Concept of Operations for Triage of Mechanical Ventilation in an Epidemic." *Society for Academic Emergency Medicine* 13 (2006): 223–29.

Hobbes, Thomas. *Leviathan*. Edited by Edwin Curley. Indianapolis: Hackett, 1994.

Homer. *Iliad*. Translated by Lang, Leaf, and Myers. New York: Macmillan, 1930.

Hume, David. *An Inquiry Concerning the Principles of Morals*. Indianapolis, IN: Hackett, 1983.

Kant, Immanuel. "Metaphysical Principles of Virtue." In *Immanuel Kant, Ethical Philosophy*, trans. James W. Ellington. Indianapolis, IN: Hackett, 1994.

Kendrick, T. D. *The Lisbon Earthquake*. London: Methuen and Co., 1956.

Klein, Naomi. *The Shock Doctrine: The Rise of Disaster Capitalism*. New York: Metropolitan Books, 2007.

Lansing, Alfred. *Endurance*. London: Weidenfeld & Nicolson, 2000.

Locke, John. *Second Treatise of Government*. In *Two Treatises of Government*, edited by Peter Laslett. New York: Cambridge University Press, 1991.

Marx, Karl, and Friedrich Engels. "The Communist Manifesto." In *Karl Marx, Selected Writings*, edited by Lawrence H. Simon. Indianapolis, IN: Hackett, 1994.

McCarthy, Cormac. *The Road*. New York: Vintage Books, Random House, 2006.

Moss, Sarah. *The Frozen Ship: The Histories and Tales of Polar Exploration*. New York: United Tribes Media, 2006.

Nielsen, Kai. "A Defense of Utilitarianism." *Ethics* 82 (1972): 113–24. Reprinted in Louis B. Pojman, ed. *The Moral Life: An Introductory Reader in Ethics and Literature*. New York: Oxford University Press, 2004, 237–51.

Pearce, Fred. *When the Rivers Run Dry: Water—The Defining Crisis of the Twenty-first Century*. Boston: Beacon Press, 2006.

Petersen, R. E. "Emergency Preparedness and Continuity of Operations (COP) in the Federal Judiciary." *Defense Technical Information Center*. Assession no. ADA446189.

Pojman, Louis B., ed. *The Moral Life: An Introductory Reader in Ethics and Literature*. New York: Oxford University Press, 2004.

Quarantelli, E. L. "Epilogue: Where We Have Been and Where We Might Go: Putting the Elephant Together, Blowing Soap Bubbles, and Having Singular Insights." In *What Is a Disaster: Perspectives on the Question*, edited by E. L. Quarantelli. London: Routledge, 1998, 234–73.

Ransby, B. "Katrina, Black Women, and the Deadly Discourse on Black Poverty in America." *DuBois Review* 3, no. 1 (spring 2006): 215–22.

Rawls, John. *A Theory of Justice*. Cambridge, MA: Belknap Press, 1971.

Rousseau, Jean-Jacques. *The Social Contract*. Edited by Maurice Cranston. New York: Penguin Classics, 1961.

Saucier, Donald A., Sara J. Smith, and Jessica L. McManus. "The Possible Role of Discrimination." *Journal of Race and Policy* 3, Special Issue, *In Katrina's Wake: Racial Implications of the New Orleans Disaster* (spring/summer 2007): 108–21.

Shackleton, Ernest. *South: The Endurance Expedition*. New York: New American Library, 1999. Reprinted from London: William Heinemann, 1919.

Spiegelman, Art. *In the Shadow of No Towers*. New York: Pantheon Books, 2004.

Teasley, Martell L. "Organizational Cultural Competence and Disaster Relief Participation." *Journal of Race and Policy* 3, Special Issue, *In Katrina's Wake: Racial Implications of the New Orleans Disaster* (spring/summer 2007): 102–12.

Thomas, James C., Nabarun Dasgupta, and Amanda Martinot. "Ethics in a Pandemic: A Survey of the State Pandemic Influenza Plans." *American Journal of Public Health* 97, no. S1 (2007): S26-31.

Veatch, Robert M. "Disaster Preparedness and Triage: Justice and the Common Good." *Mount Sinai Journal of Medicine* 72, no. 4 (2005): 236–41.

Von Winterfeldt, Detlof. "Using Risk and Decision Analysis to Protect New Orleans against Future Hurricanes." In *On Risk and Disaster: Lessons from Hurricane Katrina*, edited by Ronald J. Daniels, Donald F. Kent, and Howard Kunreuther. Philadelphia: University of Pennsylvania Press, 2006, 27–40.

Williams, Bernard. "Integrity." In "A Critique of Utilitarianism." In *Utilitarianism: For and Against*, edited by Bernard Williams and J. J. C. Smart. Cambridge, MA: Cambridge University Press, 1973.

Zack, Naomi. *Philosophy of Science and Race*. New York: Routledge, 2002.

———. "Philosophy and Disaster." *Homeland Security Affairs* 2, no. 1, art. 5 (2006): 1–2 (www.hsaj.org/?article=2.1.5).

———. "Race and Racial Discrimination." In *Oxford Handbook of Practical Ethics*, edited by Hugh Lafollette. Oxford: Oxford University Press, 2002, 2006, 245–71.

NEWSPAPER AND MAGAZINE ARTICLES

Belluck, Pam. "Glue Maker for Big Dig Is Charged in '06 Death." *New York Times*, August 9, 2007, A7.

Bond, Julian. "In Katrina's Wake," from M. Davis, "Who Is Killing New Orleans?" *The Nation*, April 10, 2006, 28–29.

———. "The Race to Rebuild: The Color of Opportunity and the Future of New Orleans." Center for Social Inclusion, August 2006, www.centerforsocialinclusion.org/PDF/racetorebuild.pdf.

Foster, Mary. "Couple Acquitted in Storm Deaths." Associated Press in *Register Guard*, September 8, 2007, A5.

Frazer, Ian. "Legacy of a Lonesome Death." *Mother Jones*, November/December 2004, www.motherjones.com/commentary/slant/2004/11/10_200.html.

Geiger, Kimberly. "New Law Puts Funds at Risk If Animals Are Not in Disaster Plans." *San Francisco Chronicle*, October 10, 2006, A-2.

Kitagawa, Manuba. "Asia: Winter Threatens to Compound Horror of Pakistani Earthquake." asahi.com, December 17, 2005, www.asahi.com.

McGee, Bill. "Focus on Terrorism May Obscure Other Airline Safety Threats." *USA Today*, October 3, 2007, www.usatoday.com/travel/columnist/mcgee/2007-10-03-airline-safety-threats_N.htm.

Nossiter, Adam. "Grand Jury Won't Indict Doctor in Hurricane Deaths." *New York Times*, July 25, 2007, www.nyytimes.com/2007/07/25/us25doctor.html_r=1&oref=slogan.

"President Bush Offers Thanksgiving Greetings." The White House. November 20, 2007. www.whitehouse.gov/news/releases/2007/11/20071119-9.html.

Wald, Matthew J. "Late Design Change Is Cited in Collapse of Tunnel Ceiling." *New York Times*, November 2, 2006, A17.

WEBSITES

Airline Passenger Rights:
  news.yahoo.com/s/ap/20071115/ap_on_go_pr_wh/airline_delays.
  http://strandedpassengers.blogsport.com.
"Altered Standards of Care in Mass Casualty Event." Contract No. 290-04-0010, pre-
  pared by Health Systems Research, Inc. AHRQ Publication No. 05-0043, April
  2005, 1–53, www.ahrq.gov/research/altstand (accessed June 2007).
Andes flight disaster. www.gdaspotlight.com/PDF/1.pdf.
Bills of Rights:
  England. www.webmesh.co.uk/englishbillofrights1689.htm.
  United Nations. www.un.org/Overview/rights.html.
  United States. www.archives.gov/national-archives-experience/charters/bill of_rights
  .html.
Bush, George W. National Security Presidential Directive/NSPD 51. Homeland Se-
  curity Presidential Directive/HSPD-20. May 9, 2007. www.whitehouse.gov/news/
  releases/2007/05/20070509-12.html. (The 2007 directive revokes its predecessor,
  Presidential Decision Directive 67. October 21, 1998. www.fas.org/irp/offdocs/
  pdd/pdd-67.htm.)
CERT. www.citizencorps.gov/cert.
Epictetus. "The Enchiridion." Translated by Elizabeth Carter. Internet Classics
  Archive. http://classics.mit.edu/Epictetus/epicench.html.
Federal Emergency Management Agency (FEMA). www.fema.gov/about/stafact
  .shtm.
Help Jet. www.helpjet.us.
Homer. *The Iliad*. Translated by Samuel Butler. Internet Classics Archives. http://
  classics.mit.edu/Homer/iliad.html.
Influenza. www.influenza.com (accessed June 2007; for U.S. residents only).
Kinlaw, Kathy, and Robert Levine. "Ethical Guidelines in Pandemic Influenza—
  Recommendations of the Ethics Subcommittee of the Advisory Committee to the
  Director." Centers for Disease Control and Prevention. February 15, 2007.
  www.cdc.gov/od/science/phec/panFlu_Ethic_Guidelines.pdf.
Milton, John. *Areopagitica: A Speech for the Liberty of Unlicensed Printing for the Par-
  liament of England.* University of Richmond. www.urich.edu/~creamer/milton/
  chron.html.
Pet Rescue.
  press_releases/president_bush_signs_pets_Act.html.
State of Louisiana v. Anna M. Pou, Lori L. Budo, and Cheri A. Landry. FindLaw. July
  2006. news.findlaw.com/usatoday/docs/katrina/lapoui706wrnt.html.
United Nations. *The 3rd United Nations World Water Development Report: Water in a
  Changing World.* March 16, 2009. www.unesco.org/water/wwap/wwdr/wwdr3.
University of Toronto Joint Centre for Bioethics Pandemic Influenza Working
  Group. "Stand on Guard for Thee: Ethical Considerations in Preparedness Plan-
  ning for Pandemic Influenza." Joint Centre for Bioethics. November 2005.
  www.utoronto.ca/jcb/home/documents/pandemic.pdf.
U.S. Public Interest Research Group. www.uspirg.org.

Index

About the Author

Naomi Zack received her Ph.D. in philosophy from Columbia University in 1970 and after a twenty-year absence from academia, began teaching at the University at Albany, SUNY, in 1990. She has been professor of philosophy at the University of Oregon since 2001. She is the author of *Race and Mixed Race* (1993), *Bachelors of Science* (1996), *Philosophy of Science and Race* (2002), *Inclusive Feminism* (2005), and the short textbook *Thinking about Race* (2nd edition, 2005). Zack is also the editor of *American Mixed Race* (1995) , *RACE/SEX* (1997), and *Women of Color and Philosophy* (2002).